And I *Held* their *Hands* with a *Hospice Heart*

Stories of Hope, Faith, Love, and Loss

SUSAN LEE MINTZ

In the memory of Dr. Jeffrey A. Mintz, 20% of the proceeds will go to hospice to assist patients and their families.

Purpose Publishing
1503 Main Street #168 ♀ Grandview, Missouri
www.purposepublishing.com

Copyright © 2016 by Susan Lee Mintz

ISBN: 978-0-9979853-9-9

Editing by Felicia Murrell
Book Cover Design by Lapridos Mairito

All rights reserved. No part of this book may be reproduced, stored in a retrieval system, or transmitted in any form or by any means; electronic, mechanical, digital, photocopy, recording, except for brief quotations in printed reviews without the permission of the publisher.

For permission and requests, write to the publisher:
1503 Main Street, #168, Grandview, MO 64030.

Author Inquiries may be sent to contactus@purposepublishing.com

Preface

"And I Held their Hands with a Hospice Heart"

Since my husband's death on August 17, 1994, I have focussed my attention and energy on the many issues involving my 25-year marriage to a man who suffered with a life-threatening illness. I assisted others who were facing many of the same issues that I had to confront. These issues involved emotions and heartfelt, sometimes gut wrenching situations where I was not only a wife, but a caregiver, friend and eventually a widow. I learned about hospice when I was told that there was nothing further that could be done for my husband. He knew he was going to die and we chose hospice to assist us. I didn't realize how important it was to have someone help me through the most difficult time in my life. Hospice was a stranger who came into our home and loved us. They understood my agony and comforted me. They helped keep the dignity and pride in my husband's life. They asked no questions and gave us unconditional support.

Because of hospice's invaluable help, I decided to give back by volunteering at Hospice By The Sea in Boca Raton, Florida. I was there for 6 incredible years working in their care center, in people's homes, and as an 11th hour patient volunteer who was called upon when death was eminent. Because I got to know many of the patients and their families, I heard powerfully incredible stories about courageous people and their remarkable spirit. Now it is time to share some of these stories with you. I hope they will encourage and inspire you through many of the most stressful and sorrowful times of your lives. Each chapter represents a common issue that many people going through these situations will deal with and/or will go through in the future. I related their stories because of my own personal experiences and understood how they felt during those challenging times.

First, let me explain what Hospice means. The word hospice is derived from the Latin "hospes," meaning host or guest, or "hospitum" meaning "guesthouse." It began in the middle ages by religious groups offering resting-places for weary or sick travelers on their long journeys. Dame Cicely Saunders founded the first modern day hospice, St. Christopher's in London in 1967. A volunteer brought the concept to Connecticut in the early 1970's. Today there are thousands of hospices in the United States.

But, what does hospice mean, not from a dictionaries' definition or an historical perspective, but from deeply heartfelt and personal experiences? Hospice is about choice. Hospice is about living and not about dying. Hospice involves choices that include dignity, respect, love, faith, and courage. Hospice doesn't treat the "terminally ill" patient. It treats the very much "living" person. When it is determined that a patient has a short-term life expectancy of 6 months or less, hospice is an alternative choice in determining how you want to live out the remaining days of your life. Hospice is concerned about one's quality of life and not about it's longevity. The physical, mental, psychological, and spiritual needs of the patient and the family are included in the hospice concept. The family is the "unit" that is treated for the disease. It is a total program of care and support and that's why it is so powerful.

As I tell you about hospice and the love I have for this organization, it shall be through stories. Personal stories and very personal people I met while I volunteered at the care center. Their stories helped me to heal after my loss because I could relate to them. As for me and the people in these stories, hospice was everything right in life when everything was wrong. When life and every aspect of it was out of control, hospice interceded and managed the chaos and turmoil. Hospice for everyone was a "team" effort and after my husband died, I joined this team. My time with hospice was certainly not the same as other people's time with them. Their circumstances, diseases, ages, settings, and so many other variables were vastly diverse from mine. But, "team hospice" rallies around the "family unit" and assists during this critical time. Sometimes it was difficult to write these stories because I knew all too well what many of these people were going through. But sometimes when you have walked the path and followed in other's footsteps, the journey is not as difficult as you might have thought. Other's strength can give you strength. Other's hope can give you hope. Other's faith can give you faith. And other's courage can give you courage. Through the following 24 stories and by publicly speaking about hospice, my mission is to share my own experiences with the similarities that many long-term/life-threatening illnesses have in common. When you think that there are no choices left, there is still one.

THE HOSPICE CHOICE
"QUALITY OF LIFE THROUGH THE END OF LIFE"

Proceeds and Dedication

20% of the proceeds from "AND I HELD THEIR HANDS WITH A HOSPICE HEART" will be donated to hospice for the care and commitment they have made for others. This book is dedicated to all those who have been in, around, and through the hospice program and for the love and understanding that hospice strives and is able to achieve. To all the patients, families, loved ones, friends, and the professional staff that assists, this book is for you. May God continue to bless you for all the great works you do and may His love shine on all those involved.

Thank you for taking such good care of my husband Dr. Jeffrey A. Mintz in his time of need. You helped maintain his dignity, his privacy, respect, and quality of life until his death on August 17, 1994. I am forever grateful.

Susan Lee Mintz

Table of Contents

Stories of Hope, Faith, Love, and Loss

This book contains 24 stories about people who have addressed issues pertaining to death, love, loss, grieving and the recovery process. It is the sequel and a companion book for my own personal story and the loss of my husband Dr. Jeffrey A. Mintz from AIDS in 1994. My book entitled "Committed To Love" detailed the gamut of emotions and circumstances I had to address and some that many of you may have to face if someone you love has a long term and/or life threatening illness. It is through these stories that I could continue to heal and go on for they speak volumes about remarkable courage, faith, hope and love. It is my wish that these stories help others in the future for this book as well as mine is informational, motivational, and inspirational. These are true stories that include hospice patients, their families, friends, and the professional personnel who assisted them. Their experiences included life altering situations and involved making difficult choices. However, through the most challenging of times, these stories epitomized and represented the strength and faith that is the hospice philosophy.

"QUALITY OF LIFE THROUGH THE END OF LIFE."

Chapter 1   He Was Staying Involved Until The End As He Sang Spanish Hymns To His Dying Mother   15

Chapter 2   He Finally Had The Truth About His Illness And Now He Could Deal With The Facts Because He Knew Them 25

Chapter 3   Their Love, Devotion, And Maintaining A Sense Of Humor Gave Them The Strength To Go On As 2 Sisters Lost Both Parents Within 24 Hours   35

Chapter 4   Care Giving Comes In Many Forms And Many Ways And For This Man It Was All About His Love For Chocolate Chip Cookies   45

Chapter 5   Feeling Guilty Doesn't Do Any Good-But Sometimes It's The Only Thing You Will Feel And For This Daughter Who Thought She Was Crying Because She Was Weak It Was Just The Opposite   55

Chapter 6   After His Tragic Year A Son Questions Whether He Will Ever Have Fun, Laugh, Or Feel Alive Again   65

Chapter 7 As A Wife Sat Reading Her Bible Praying For Peace, She Was Caught In A Catch 22 For She Was Cherishing Every Moment While Wishing This Time Was Over 73

Chapter 8 A Wife Questions How She Will Start Over After Her Husband's Death and What She Will Do With Her Time Alone
81

Chapter 9 When A Life Threatening Illness Tested The Power Of His Faith He Envied Those Who Truly Believed in God 91

Chapter 10 As Her Father Was Dying She Said That It Reminded Her Of Her Child At Birth-It Was A Complete 360 And The Totality Of The Cycle Of Life 101

Chapter 11 There Was No Safe Place or Comfort Zone As A Hospice Nurse Said She Was Afraid To Bring Her Baby Home And A Wife Who Expressed The Same Concerns About Her Husband
111

Chapter 12 A Wife Who Feels Like She Is Starving Her Husband To Death But He Doesn't Have The Strength, Energy, Or Appetite To Eat 121

Chapter 13 How A Breast Cancer Survivor For 15 Years Was Able To Focus On The Present And Enjoy Every Day That She Had Left
131

Chapter 14 A Daughter Questions Her Fears As She Faces The Issue Is She More Afraid To Leave Her Loved One Or To Come Back 141

Chapter 15   Pain Comes In Many Ways But For This Woman The Physical Pain Of Her Illness Was So Horrible That She Wanted To Commit Suicide   149

Chapter 16   A Woman With Terminal Lung Cancer Had To Slowly Give Up Everything She Loved But She Managed To Have Fun And Keep Some Control By Having Her Daily Cigarette And Would Smoke Until She Could Never Hold A Cigarette Again
                                                                                       159

Chapter 17   How A Hospice Nurse Was Able To Separate Her Personal Life From Her Professional One As She Dealt With Her Husband's Illness And Death And Came Back To Hospice To Help Others   169

Chapter 18   A Woman Converted To Catholicism At The Care Center And Said That Until Her Last Breath It Was Never To Late To Make Something Good Happen   177

Chapter 19   A Wife Who Had To Talk To Her Sister About Dying Because Her Husband Could Not Deal With It And She Didn't Understand Why It Was So Hard That They Couldn't   187

Chapter 20   This Man Thought That He Was In Control Of His Emotions After His Mother Died But He Had Not Taken The Necessary Time To Grieve And His Emotional Waves Finally Caught Up With Him   197

Chapter 21   The Effects Of A Long Term Illness Can Be Difficult For The Entire Family And For This Woman She Didn't Want To Be A Burden To The Ones She Loved Any Longer   207

Chapter 22   This Woman Felt That She Caused Her Husband's Illness And Was Responsible For Everything But Her Feelings Of Guilt And Anger Didn't Do Any Good Nor Could It Change Anything   217

Chapter 23   This Woman Felt That The Treatment Was Worse Than The Disease And She Chose To Have Quality Of Life Rather Than Suffer Through The Treatments   227

Chapter 24   A Son Comes To His Father's Deathbed Out Of Respect But It Was Not Because He Loved Him   237

About the Author   247

Chapter 1

He Was Staying Involved Until the End as He Sang Spanish Hymns to His Dying Mother

"It's called the needing to be needed need."

June 1998

Dear Jeff,

I realized that most of my writing was done early in the morning. By 9:00 a.m. the sun was shining brilliantly on the balcony of our home and I basked in the warmth and serenity of that time. I watched the world around me come to life and my thoughts ran freely through an uncluttered mind. Though my writing continued to be my therapy, it also became my best friend. It was difficult adjusting to the new life I had to make for myself after your death Jeffrey, but I had finally healed and ultimately grown through the tragedy of your illness. I now could say that I had come to terms with my past and look forward with renewed optimism to the future. But Jeff, you never knew why I wrote my stories because you were already gone. I wrote because through hospice I met the most courageous and inspirational people who shared their heartwarming touching experiences and that enabled me to keep the bridge between us open. Your spirit lived through the people in these stories and it is that link that shall never be broken. The following stories have become the bridge that shall keep us together forever.

My volunteer responsibilities at hospice were quite simple and easy, but they were important and meaningful because I assisted the patient or family member in any way I could. It was very rewarding to know that people appreciated my care and concern during their difficult time. It's ironic that while during someone's greatest time of need, his or her needs are really sadly simple and few. However, I was privileged to be able to share the end of their journey with them. These men and women were total strangers to me, yet we were bound together by our faith and trust in hospice. I remain grateful for the opportunity to have been able to give comfort and support to someone else as they said their good-byes to those they loved. The common thread between these people and myself was that they wanted reassurance. They wanted to be told that their strength and courage during this difficult time would eventually be worth it. As they shared their feelings, they spoke openly and candidly about personal problems and painfully emotional issues. Thus began my journey into the lives of the people in the following 24 stories. Their stories were our stories and their lives were our lives. We shared lives.

I was looking forward to my volunteer shift that Monday night because I'd been feeling restless for a few days. The care center always settled my spirit down because hospice somehow managed to keep me focused on what was really important. Hospice was about life and not about death. The atmosphere there renewed my energy and the evening hours were quiet and peaceful. I liked the beginning of my shift because I brought fresh ice and water into the patients' rooms. Delivering water was an easy non-threatening way to approach a family while entering into their private space. It was vitally important to respect the patient's privacy and not put anyone in an awkward situation. It also gave me the opportunity to ask if someone needed anything special or perhaps the patient wanted company.

It was on that one special night when I saw a soft mystical shadow of flickering candlelight coming from a corner room. As I watched the flames dancing through the hallway, I heard a man's voice so magnificent that I thought it was coming from a radio or tape. I stood motionless outside the door leaning against the wall as I listened to the voice of an angel. I tapped lightly on the door and walked into the room. In front of me were a dozen people sitting in a circle around the bed keeping a watchful and tearful vigil over their loved one's body. The tables were filled with small flower arrangements and there were family pictures everywhere. Religious figurines and ornaments cast a heavenly spell over this man made church. Everyone was holding a golden rosary and chanting along with the man. I felt honored to be sharing their sacred place with a woman who was so blessed in life as well as in her eventual passing.

I asked the family if I could stay. Though they spoke very little English, their warm smiles and nodding gestures made me feel welcomed. The man with the angelic voice was around 30 years of age. His slender body looked small and frail as the candle's shadows danced around the room. He was half sitting, half leaning over the bed with a prayer book resting in his hands. His mother slept peacefully taking soft shallow breaths as she continued to stay alive. Her husband held her hand and gently stroked her brow. The soft caring touch of his hand did not cause her to move or change the expression on her face. I believed that she could hear her son's voice and feel her husband's warmth, but she was in her own special place and no one would know what she could hear or understand.

He touched my soul as he sang his Spanish hymns and psalms to his dying mother. He was pouring out his love and devotion to her through the words in the prayers and the emotions in their meaning. I could hear the heartache in his voice and saw the tears streaming down his cheeks, but his soothing voice brought peace and comfort to everyone. I did not understand his words or the psalms he sang, but I wanted to share this time with them. I needed to share their sadness and their loss. I wanted the music to make me cry. But I also wanted to rejoice in their faith and feel the power of their love, because love was the one thing that held them together. They were celebrating life, living, and a family's bond. It was the purest and simplest thing I'd ever seen.

Her family wanted her to feel that power and her son wanted to make their last moments together as beautiful as possible. He couldn't do anything to prevent her death, but he did everything to make her feel alive. He was doing what he thought would bring her the greatest pleasure and he was also doing something important and necessary for himself. As difficult and emotional as those last few hours were, "his needing to be needed need" instinctively continued. It's that "wanting to be needed feeling that never stops." It is a feeling that may not go away after your loved one has died. I wept both tears of sadness and joy with a beautiful family last night. During my 4 hours at the center, he never stopped singing to his mother.

It was 11:00 PM but I wasn't ready to go home. As I poured myself a cup of coffee, I tried to figure out why tonight's experience had such a powerful impact on me. Why did the music touch me the way it did? And why did his gentle voice bring back so many bittersweet memories of another time when the music played and the warm glow of candlelight filled the room? After a while, I remembered why I felt the way I did. The music and his singing took me back to Austria and the beautiful vacation we never got to enjoy. I remember everything as clearly as if it happened yesterday. It was May 1994 and you had planned a two-week motor trip throughout Austria. Though we had traveled extensively throughout Europe, we never made it to this magnificent country with its splendor, history, and Old World charm. I wanted to eat my way through the picturesque countryside and attend the Opera every night listening to Strauss Waltzes and Mozart Concertos.

Yes, tonight a young man's voice took me back to Austria and the beautiful dance called the waltz. I danced in my heart and came alive as I was catapulted back in time and our last few days together. Though everything he was doing was totally different than what I had done, we shared the same feelings and tried to make it better for someone we loved. Jeff we desperately needed this trip to lift our spirits and we wanted to have something positive to look forward to. But, when you were stricken with your third bout of pneumonia, we were forced to cancel our plans. This time the pneumonia weakened you so terribly that you weren't able to fight back. Your health deteriorated very quickly and by August we knew your death was eminent. That was when I knew there was something I could do to make us feel like we were in Austria together. Oh how I wanted to thank this man for helping me remember what I did and may this story help others who want to keep their "needing to be needed need" never ending.

One afternoon while our hospice aide was with you, I went out and bought a dozen CD's of Strauss Waltzes and Mozart Concertos. I closed my eyes and listened to the beautiful music in the store and I felt your arms holding me tightly as we danced our favorite waltz under a starlit romantic sky. I wanted to hold onto that picture forever. When I arrived home, your parents and a few friends were with you. Everyone left around 8:00 PM and I said, "Jeffrey, I have a surprise for you. We are going to take our Austrian vacation now." I turned off all the lights and lit candles everywhere. I put the first CD on and we listened as the passionate music flowed throughout our room. The soothing rhythm took us away from the cruel reality of this horrible time.

I held your hand and we pretended that we were waltzing in Vienna under a moonlit Austrian sky. The setting in the bedroom was magnificent and the atmosphere created celebrated your life and not your death. Everyone who came to visit could feel the positive energy surrounding you. You were enveloped in a blanket of love, beauty, dignity, and pride. The music played endlessly for two days and on August 17th I turned off those beautiful Viennese waltzes. I don't know if the music made you feel like you were in Austria, but I hope that for a little while you were "somewhere splendidly clean and deliciously healthy." I'd like to think that we were together just like we planned. Maybe I did this for myself more than I did it for you. But, I wanted to keep you in my life a little longer and my "needing to be needed need" was all that mattered. I am thankful that time always has a way of putting things into perspective.

About 2 months before you passed away you said to me, "Susan, I am not afraid to die." "What do you mean by that?" I asked? You said, "My life is simpler and easier now, because it's out of my control. It doesn't matter what we try to do any longer. I am going to die. All the obstacles have been removed and my journey is right on schedule. I have nothing left to prove and everything has worked out the way it was supposed to do. Or, perhaps the way it had to. That's what makes life so different than death. There are no more choices or decisions to make and no plans to constantly change. Dying is life in its most simplistic form. My diagnosis forced me to confront honestly and openly my bisexuality. We have resolved our conflicts as husband and wife and individually as wonderful people who loved each other. You have helped me face my worst fears and in the process you have also faced yours. I have come to terms with myself and I've cherished every moment of our unconventional relationship. Thank you for loving me."

You fell asleep holding my hands. Yes, my love, last night at the care center, the singing young man made a powerful and lingering impression on me. Thanks for allowing me to share it with you.

I'll say so long for a little while.

I love you.

Susan

Chapter 2

He Finally Had The Truth About His Illness And
Now He Could Deal With The Facts Because He Knew Them

"You can take control of your life, but you can't control it."

July 1998,

Dear Jeff,

Why do I sometimes forget the things I want to remember and remember the things I wish to forget? It's very difficult for me to describe the deeply powerful and emotional flashbacks that I've been having since your death. They happen often and without warning. In an instant, something someone says or does will shift my attention from the present and take me back to the past. Everything I see now is totally different, yet the things I remember feel frighteningly familiar. It is impossible for me to control these vivid images that come to mind. Jeff, when my memories are beautiful, I am thankful for the wondrous feelings they bring to me. I cherish the incredible adventure we shared. Unfortunately, there are other times when I am reminded of the terribly frustrating and challenging things we also faced. These memories are painful ones to relive, but they were a part of our life. Learning how to acknowledge and accept both the good and the bad memories was a difficult thing for me to do. Last night at the care center, I experienced something that brought back the feelings and images that were both bitter and sweet.

When I started my shift, it was unusually quiet. The rooms were only half occupied and there were very few visitors around. I loaded my cart up with ice, cups, straws and napkins and proceeded to deliver fresh water to the patient's rooms. As I turned the corner, I noticed a large powerfully built man leaning against the wall. He was staring into the empty hallway and continued to watch me walk towards him. His presence and stature caught me off guard and I thought that he was visiting someone else. He looked like a sentry posted outside the room. As I got closer, I saw the oxygen line hooked up to a portable tank near his side. But, there was something different about him that captured my attention. He looked exactly like the man in a painting that we almost bought at the Norman Rockwell Museum almost 10 years ago. I stopped the cart in front of him and said, "Wow, what a treat. Someone up and walking! I don't see that very much around here!"

Jeff, he laughed so hard that the oxygen tube went flying out of his nose. He adjusted his nosepiece and slapped me on the back. "Well done," he said. I responded, "Would you like some company? It's quiet around here tonight and I've got a lot of time." He answered, "Yes, and if you bring me a couple cups of strong black high octane coffee, I'll really talk your head off." I said, "Don't go away and I'll bring you the whole pot."

He was sitting up in bed when I got back to the room. A pink sign had been neatly scotch taped on the door. It read, DO NOT CLOSE THE DOORS OR DRAW THE CURTAINS. I proceeded to put the coffee on the night table and pulled a white wicker chair up along side his bed. "Hi again, I said. My name is Susan and I'm your lucky volunteer tonight." I asked him if he really wanted some company or did he prefer to be alone. He said, "Susan, I like the purple turban you are wearing. You look very exotic." I said, "You, my friend, have great taste in women." He laughed nodding his head in approval. I noticed his dinner tray hadn't been touched and said, "How's the food in this hotel?" He said, "Well if I could breathe long enough to chew the mashed potatoes, I could tell you!" We both giggled like small children who were keeping a secret from their parents. There was something about his honesty and sense of humor that made me feel at ease. I pulled the chair closer to the bed and asked him about the sign on the door. "Are you claustrophobic," I said. He never answered my question.

He took a few sips of coffee and adjusted his oxygen line. Then he said, "Susan, you can only deal with the facts that you know." An unsettling uneasy feeling came over me. Where had I heard those words before? My heart raced and my mind went blank. A moment later, all I could think about was you Jeff. Those were the same words you said to me after your third bout with pneumonia. I didn't know how to respond. Finally I said, "That was a powerful statement you just made. Honesty and being told the truth are the most important things in life. Everything we are told to believe in is a lie without them." He took his coffee and got into the recliner. He said, "I told everyone that my coping mechanism finally shorted out. I think that I was given too much information too quickly. I was overloaded with test results and opinions. I was frustrated because a lot of the information I received about my condition wasn't correct. Maybe I didn't ask the right questions of the right people. It wasn't anyone's fault. But, how could I make the right decisions when I didn't know all the facts? I was tired of the half-truths, the guesswork, and the speculation. That's what frustrated me the most. I wasn't given the correct information until it was too late. Now that I know the truth about my illness and the prognosis, I can finally take charge of my life again. Yes, you can only deal with what you know. I've made peace with myself and everyone else."

He wanted to get back into bed. I asked him if he was tired and if I should leave. "No, he said, you're a good listener." Now I was the one who laughed out loud. I said, "That's the most wonderful compliment you could have given me. People are always telling me that I talk too much and don't listen." He continued, "I'm 65 years old and my wife and I still work. I wanted to come into the center because my wife is not handling my illness well. I love her very much and would like to be at home, but I can't right now. I need some peace and quiet and she won't give me that. She is angry with everyone, including myself, and blames the doctors for my illness." Again, that strange uneasy feeling came over me. My mind went blank. Then my thoughts were back with you. I remembered the times when I wasn't able to cope with your illness either and took my anger and frustrations out on you and everyone else who cared about us. I know that there were times when my horrible attitude made your life more unbearable than it already was. I am sorry for not having been as understanding and tolerant as I should have been. His voice interrupted my thoughts startling me back to our conversation. He said, "You understand what I am talking about, don't you?" "All too well," I said.

He continued, "I've been a heavy cigarette smoker for many years. I have diabetes and had several heart attacks. It's only because I'm so damn big and strong that nothing could take me out." He chuckled at himself and said, "About a year ago, I went to my doctor complaining of severe back pain. After dozens of tests, x-rays, and consultations, the doctor determined that there wasn't anything wrong. I spent 2 months running to different hospitals, getting second and third opinions while nothing was showing up. I was angry because no one was giving me a straight answer. I had lots of information but no diagnosis. The more the doctors tried to find the reason for my pain, the less I understood and the worst I felt. The pain was excruciating. One night I woke up and couldn't breathe. I thought I was having another heart attack. My wife called 911. A chest x-ray determined that I had fluid in both lungs. I was operated on immediately and told that a lot of fluid was removed from both lungs. My doctor said that this would alleviate my condition and discharged me. When I asked how something like this can happen, he could not be specific. I accepted his opinion and thought that my problems were over.

A few weeks later the same thing happened. I went to the hospital again. This time the x-rays revealed that a tumor had wrapped itself around my heart. The results of a biopsy indicated that I had cancer of the lungs with 5 different kinds of cells. Another specialist told me that 3 of the cancers didn't have any treatment and the other 2 might respond to chemotherapy. If the treatments were successful, I might have 6 months to a year to live. My wife and I were frantic. Why didn't someone see this earlier? I felt like I had been deceived. I got very depressed, but decided to try the chemotherapy. I wanted to believe that the treatments would buy me some time. Halfway through my first chemotherapy treatment I went into cardiac arrest. I was revived and told that the treatments would have to be stopped because of my heart condition. The doctor said I had 3 months or less to live. I had prepared myself for 6 months to a year. It took me so long to get a diagnosis and honest answers to my problems and now I had to prepare for something else. I had even less time than I thought I had. My doctor said my only choice left was hospice." After that he said that he was ready to go to sleep and asked me to come back and visit with him again. As I walked out the door 2 hours later he said, "Wear another color turban next time. I like it. Good night." I turned off his light and left. He went back home 3 days later and I never saw him again.

I couldn't stop thinking about the man who reminded me of the Norman Rockwell painting. He spoke candidly about his fears and the disappointments he'd experienced throughout his illness. Everything he said reminded me of you and the frustrations you faced as you dealt with similar situations. I told him about the times when no one knew if your medications or treatments would work. How overwhelming the feelings of disappointment were when procedures had to be changed or tests hadn't been accurately done. I understood how difficult it was when the facts and statistics didn't tell us what we wanted to know. I knew how frightening it was when things didn't turn out the way we had hoped. And just like this man, you had resolved yourself to the one and only thing you could accept. It was that many times your expectations unfortunately and sadly had to be changed. However, it was his feelings about honesty and truth that kept playing over and over again in my mind. They were the most important things we asked of each other and everyone else. What I will remember most about this courageous man was that he wasn't angry or bitter now. He really didn't blame anyone for what happened. We agreed that there are some questions in life that didn't have any answers. You can only handle what you know and having the honest facts can make handling the truth much easier to accept.

I'll say so long for a little while.

I love you.

Susan

Chapter 3

Their Love, Devotion, And Maintaining A Sense Of Humor Gave Them The Strength To Go On As 2 Sisters Lost Both Parents Within 24 Hours

"She said that they were more than a family. They were friends."

August 1998,

Dear Jeff,

Last night I met 2 sisters who epitomized everything that living and loving was all about. I watched in awe as a family ran the gamut of emotions from heartache to hope, from laugher to tears. They inspired me with their sense of humor and never-ending commitment to their parents and each other. Tonight I was fortunate to have shared this experience with a wonderful woman and her two courageous daughters. I went to the care center and started my shift. There were many visitors and all the rooms were full. As I proceeded down the hallway, I noticed that the door to this room was closed. A sign was posted on it that read, "BEWARE OF DOG." I had never seen that on a door at the center before.

When I knocked I heard a soft voice telling me to come in. I hesitated at first thinking that some huge ferocious animal was going to attack me. When I went in, I was surprised to see a small white poodle nestled under the lady's arm. The woman smiled and said, "She's a holy terror when she hasn't had her wine."

My laugh disturbed the little animal that rested comfortably at the woman's side. He barked at me several times and then settled back down on a crimson pillow. I said, "It always catches me off guard when I see an animal in the room. Having your buddy here makes it feel more like home. We want you to feel that way because that's a very important part of the hospice philosophy. My name is Susan and I'm a volunteer on the floor tonight! Can I get your dog something to eat or perhaps he or she would like a drink of water?" The frail woman took a slow deep breath and said, "No, he already ate my dinner and my daughters are bringing us some wine." We laughed and the poodle started to bark again. I said, "You have a wonderful sense of humor and I am sure your dog does too." I put the water pitcher on the night table and pulled my chair up next to her bed.

I noticed that the woman had the most beautiful hands. Her nails looked freshly manicured in a bright cherry red gloss that accentuated her long slender fingers. Their elegant look was in sharp contrast to the thin fragile body before me. As I put my hand out to pet the dog, I noticed that his nails were painted too. She said, "He thinks he's a she." I said to her, "Your nails are incredible. Forgive me for saying this but they are real, aren't they?" She put both her hands up in front of her face and proudly said, "Other than my daughters and the furry third child, they are my greatest treasures. I have my mother to thank for them." I said, "If you need a touch up, I would be happy to oblige. I don't think I can do your sidekick's." She said that a friend was coming in tomorrow to do her hair and nails.

I asked her if I could stay until her family arrived. She said, "We would love the company. It is difficult for me to talk and breathe at the same time, but I want to do both as long as I can. I must use the oxygen and I have to pause often to catch my breath." I began petting the dog that was half-asleep under the blanket. She said, "I'm 66 years old. I've had advanced emphysema and lung cancer for years. I'm not in any pain, but I don't have any energy." She took several deep breaths and said, "My mind is in much better shape than my body." Gradually an understanding, almost like a rhythm, developed between us. She would speak, pause, take a few deep breaths, and continue. I said, "How can a little lady like you have such long fingers?" She said, "I am 5'8" tall and looked really good when I could stand up. I made quite a statement in my time." "Well, I said, even lying down and all bunched up, you are still making quite a statement."

I was totally unprepared for what she told me next. She said, "My husband is in another hospital. He had a heart attack after I came in here. My two daughters are with him now. They are very close with their father." I was speechless. This woman was spending her last days battling lung cancer at a hospice center while her husband was in another facility with a serious heart condition. I said, "Your daughters have quite a full plate." She acknowledged my comment by stating, "You remind me of my best friend of 40 years. She was the only woman I knew who could wear a turban and look beautiful." I told her that I wear them a lot at the center because they do not look "medical." Would you like me to take it off and show you what I really look like under this bonnet?" "Oh yes, she said. My friend had bright orange hair and to this day I don't know why she wanted to cover it up." I knew when I took off my turban and showed her my orange hair, it would make her day. I removed the purple turban and when she saw that my hair was indeed bright orange, she burst out laughing.

Unfortunately, she couldn't catch her breath and started to cough and choke at the same time. The dog got upset and started to howl and that's when her daughters arrived. It was an awkward situation for a few minutes, but eventually everything settled down. After the introductions were made, we all started to laugh. They brought in a bottle of red wine and poured it into 3 Styrofoam cups. The dog had his own little bowl. He was affectionately referred to as their other sibling with fur. They asked me if I wanted to stay and have a drink with them. I said that I was on duty, but perhaps another time. As I left, the dog was finishing his second bowl of wine. I was making coffee when the sisters came out of the room. One of the daughters was identical to her mother. She said, "Mom likes you a lot." I told her that the feeling was mutual. When I asked how their father was doing, they both snickered and half-grinned at the same time. The other daughter said, "Well, he's in worse shape than Mom. He doesn't know just how bad she is and that she's in hospice and she doesn't know that he probably won't pull through his heart attack."

I couldn't even begin to comprehend the magnitude of their pain and suffering. In disbelief I said, "You're telling me that both of your parents are gravely ill and that they might not make it through the next few weeks?" In a gentle, calm, unwavering tone, they responded in unison, "Yes." The daughter who looked like her mom said, "Neither of them can know about the severity of the other's condition and we are going to keep it that way. They are not to know how bad it really is." They went back to the room to check on their mother. A few minutes later, the look a like daughter took the dog for a walk while the other sister came back to have coffee with me. She said, "My sister and I have always been close. She's my best friend. We are devoted to each other and we've always had a great relationship with both our parents. We are more than a family. We are all friends. Our parents have been married for 37 years and they have never been apart. Now they may never see each other again."

Her concern for both of them was so genuine and sincere. She said, "My sister and I made a pact to protect our parents from any further heartache. I know that we are going to loose both of them very soon. We are trying to remain positive though it is very difficult. There have been times when I am afraid, question, and ask "why me?" But, it is less painful to say, "why not me" instead. Rationalizing and philosophizing does help sometimes." The sister came back in with the dog and sat down with us. I said, "Would the sibling with fur like a cookie and a cup of coffee?" "Yes, she said. He likes chocolate chips." They brought the dog back to the room. Mom was asleep but they didn't want to leave. The look a like daughter said, "We've been running double duty back and forth between both places for a week. I don't know how we are keeping up with this, but we are. Having each other helps." I said, "So what do you do for fun and relaxation?" They thought that was funny and in unison they said, "You haven't heard anything yet."

The daughter who didn't look like the mother said, "Want to hear about the eviction from the apartment and the lawsuit against our business?" "Sure, I said, go for it." She said, "We have to find a new apartment. We are being evicted because of the dog. There are no pets allowed where we live, but we can not give him up. We are also being sued because of a business venture that went belly up. It happened a year ago, but they have decided to sue us now. We have no place to live, no business left, and both parents are going to pass away. So, that's that. End of story." I said, "I've never heard anything like this before. How are you managing to go on? You both are so optimistic and strong." The look a like daughter said, "We don't have any choice now. This is the way it is. We have each other and we will somehow manage to get through this. We've shed plenty of tears and questioned our beliefs many times, but we have to be here for our parents now."

We said our good-byes and they left. I came back to visit with them several times during the week. Most of the time, the girls were there. They continued to remain positive, strong, and never lost their sense of humor. Though they had so much sorrow and suffering in their lives, their only concerns were for their parents, never for themselves. They inspired everyone around them and brought comfort and hope to anyone whose life they touched. As ill as the woman was, I never heard any of them complain. All I saw was the life of a beautiful lady and the devotion of a family who loved each other. One afternoon before the daughters arrived, the woman asked me why I got involved with hospice. I didn't go into detail but I told her that you had a long-term illness and how hospice helped us. I realized then why this family made such an impression on me. I said, "One of the things I always tried to do was to keep a positive attitude, even though it was nearly impossible to do. My concerns were only for my husband. It was not the time for me to think about myself. I tried to keep it all in perspective and make the precious time we had left as bearable at it could be." This family justified how important remaining positive was no matter how horrible the situation. They gave me hope and reinforced my belief that people will do what's good and right no matter how unfair life may be. Both parents passed away within 24 hours of each other. They called me to say thank you and wished me good luck.

I'll say so long for a little while.

I love you.

Susan

Chapter 4

Care Giving Comes In Many Forms And Many Ways And For This Man It Was All About His Love For Chocolate Chip Cookies

"To feel the warmth of flesh on flesh is life."

September 1998

Dear Jeff,

It's been four years since your death and I think I've finally settled into my new life without you. I've needed this time to help me prioritize and focus on what it is that I want out of life. I know that helping people through my hospice work will continue to be an integral part of the things I do in the future. For those in need of comfort and understanding during this difficult time, I will give whatever I can because I know that it will be greatly accepted and appreciated. I've also become very realistic about what I am capable of giving to myself and to others. My life now is both exciting and frightening at the same time. Though I try to keep things simple, I still manage to complicate the issues at hand. How many times did you say to me, "Susan, you are making problems for yourself that don't exist? You are your own worst enemy but you won't change." I would respond, "Thank you for the compliment." Well, I haven't changed but I did find out something very important. I've learned that the only person I have to prove anything to is myself, and that I'm the only one who can make the changes in my life that need to be made.

There is a quality of life through the end of life, but I didn't truly understand the power and importance of this until you were gone. I was too caught up in a vicious cycle of having to face your death and the denial of knowing how painful it would be afterwards. Though there is much sadness and sorrow at the care center, I see it as a place where the feelings of life and love are everywhere. It is a haven where people are treated with dignity and respect. Hospice helped me find the healing place within my heart and has enabled me to grow and understand myself so much more. What makes the human touch capable of saying what words can not? How can the touch of a hand tell someone that you care, that they are special, and that you understand what they are feeling? I remember the numerous times throughout our marriage when I told you that when you held my hand I felt more intimacy than when we were making love. When I curled up into your arms at night, I felt safe and at peace. How many times when you were afraid did my touch lessen your fears? When your raging fevers caused you to shake so violently that I feared for your safety, wasn't it my body on yours that helped to ease your suffering?

The human touch can sooth a saddened heart and bring peace to a troubled mind. The human touch is necessary because life requires of us to feel the warmth of flesh on flesh. Last week, something happened that I must share with you, because it was one of the most valuable learning experiences I've ever had. It involved the power of the human touch and a simple act of kindness. I never thought that the touch of my hand could have such a powerful impact. It was so simple and innocent, but it was profoundly meaningful and it affected me deeply. It was a warm and balmy evening when I arrived at the care center. The breezes were beautiful and some of the patio doors to the patient's rooms were open. As I knocked and entered this room, I noticed that the only light coming in was from the patio. The room looked tidy and clean, simple and homey. Was this a hospice room or a motel room? For a little while, they were one in the same.

Because of the darkness, I did not see the man tucked neatly underneath the covers in bed. I went over to put on the small table lamp when he said, "Hi, mam." The other reason why I didn't see him in the dim light was because his skin color was very dark. I said, "You startled me. I didn't see you there. Were you playing hide and seek with me? It is so dark in your room that you blended in nicely. My name is Susan and I'm a volunteer. Can I get you something?" He hesitated at first as if he didn't want to intrude on my time or inconvenience me. Then he said, "Would you please shut the doors and put another light on. I really don't like the nights. The darkness frightens me." "Sure, I said. Want the air on too?" He said in a soft weakened voice, "No, I'm okay. I like it warm." I put another light on and he said, "Thank you mam." There was a peaceful air about him that made me comfortable and I liked the way he called me "mam." He had a soft Southern accent that made me feel special.

He was wearing a beige knit cap on his hairless head. His large brown-framed reading glasses were resting comfortably on the bony bridge of his nose. There were several pictures on the tables, some with children, and others with adults. A single red rose was half-opened in a white vase, while a few bananas continued to overly ripen on a plate. A pretty coffee mug that said "Get Well Soon" was filled to the brim with chocolate kisses. The silver heart shaped balloon tied to a chair read, "We Miss You." I was so interested in the personal things that it took me some time before I realized that he was hooked up to all sorts of machines. He had monitors, IV bags, and tubes coming in and out of everywhere. I said, "Do you think you have enough gadgets to play with? You've been through a lot haven't you?" He laughed and softly said, "Yes, mam." His lips were parched and dry and I didn't know if he had the energy to eat or drink, but I said, "I just made a fresh pot of coffee with a lot of caffeine to boost you out of your bed. I spiked the cookies with extra chocolate chips, too." Well, you would have thought that I said you're well enough to take that cruise you've always wanted to go on. His face lit up and he grinned from ear to ear. He said, "Yes, mam, I'd love a few cookies."

How could something as simple as offering someone a cookie have made him so happy? Jeff, I can't explain the feeling I had when I heard his words. A few minutes later, I'd wrapped three chocolate chip cookies up in a napkin. When I went to give him the cookies, I realized that I didn't know where I could put them. He could not sit up and I couldn't rearrange his tubes, cords, and machines. Sensing my dilemma he said, "Please put them on my stomach." "Okay, I said, but no crumbs in bed or we'll discontinue the midnight snacks." I placed the napkin with the three chocolate cookies on his belly. He devoured the first one. I said, "Well, we are real friends now. Chocolate does it everytime. Would you like some company? I could stay and visit for a while?" "Yes, he said. Will you bring me some more if we run out?" "Oh yes, I said, as many as you want."

I pulled the white wicker chair over and lowered the side rail of the bed. We didn't talk about very much but that didn't matter to either of us. He just wanted some company and a couple of chocolate chip cookies. I was just sitting there hoping that he would ask for more. We were only together for about 30 minutes but we had done something special that made us both feel good. We were two strangers who bonded over a few chocolate chip cookies and we were giving care to each other. These few minutes would not affect the end results, but how this man lives until the end is what I cared about. The cookies changed nothing but they made all the difference in the world to us.

I went back to the center a week later to see how he was doing. When I knocked and went into the room, I could tell by his smile that he was happy to see me. The tubes had been removed from his body and the medical equipment taken from the room. His beige baseball cap and dark glasses were just as they had been a week ago. His condition had gotten much worse but he was still aware of what was going on around him. As I came closer to the bed, his smile gave way to a giggle. "Hi, he said. Mam do have any more of those chocolate chip cookies?" He was grinning from ear to ear. I was smiling back at him with tears in my eyes. I took his hands in mine and said, "You remembered." In the most sincere and appreciative voice I had ever heard he said, "Of course, I remembered." It was an overwhelming experience and I started to cry. I was relieved knowing that I had to go and get the cookies, because I needed some time to compose myself. I found a white paper napkin and wrapped three chocolate chip cookies up in it. When I got back to the room, I placed them neatly in the middle of his stomach.

As I sat stroking this sweet man's forehead, he told me over and over again about how simple and easy his life had become. I stayed with him until his pain medication took effect and he fell asleep. Tonight, he didn't eat the chocolate chip cookies. They just rested on his stomach as if they had found a home. One day I would go back and his bed would be empty, but I will never look at a chocolate chip cookie the same way again. It has taken me a long time to understand that there is a sense of order in life and in death. When I hear grieving relatives and friends use words like weak, raw, numb, and vulnerable to express how they feel now, all I can do is to try and reassure them that they are strong and courageous, and that they will work through their loss in time. But, while their loved one is still in their life, just a simple touch, a gentle caress, and the warmth of flesh on flesh can make all the difference in the world.

A simple act of kindness can make the heartache a little more bearable and the memories more beautiful. The human touch is a powerful energy force that binds people together through the good times and the bad. I am glad that I was able to give care to a beautiful man who shared a few chocolate chip cookies and his life with me. What is the difference between care giving and giving care? Nothing. There is nothing different at all. Dearest Jeff, we gave and received a lot of both during our 25 years together and I thank you for letting me take care of you and thank you for the many tender acts of kindness you gave to me. Chocolate chip cookies were your favorite ones, too.

I'll say so long for a little while.

I love you.

Susan

Chapter 5

Feeling Guilty Doesn't Do Any Good-But Sometimes It's The Only Thing You Will Feel And For This Daughter Who Thought She Was Crying Because She Was Weak It Was Just The Opposite

"Passion and tears are kindred spirits. To know life is to cry."

October 1998

Dear Jeff,

We used to talk for hours about everything, anything, or nothing at all, and we always agreed on the important things, didn't we? We shared a special communication that very few people will ever know. Something happened last night at the care center that made me realize that I hadn't always been as honest and open with you as I could have been. I didn't talk to you about "me." There were many feelings and emotions I didn't know about until you became ill and died. How could I tell you about myself when so much of me hadn't even happened yet? I've had to explore my own beliefs and learn to face myself, but I've had to do this on my own. I couldn't have been honest with you until I found out how to be honest with myself first? Through my hospice experiences and by living without you, I am learning how to face my own personal issues and deal with things that have frightened me in the past. I will write to you about feelings and emotions and tell you about the woman you never knew. I will continue to explore these new and unfamiliar aspects of my life, but I will do this self-exploration through my writing. Through written words and other people's stories we will stay together.

Last night at the care center, I saw a young woman crying at the bedside of her dying mother. As I watched her holding the lady's hand, I felt a tear run down my cheek. I didn't know why I was crying but I was. Why? What other reasons could there be to get me to react this way? I wasn't sad or in pain. I wasn't cold, hungry, or tired. Why was I crying? I was crying because I loved. And what I was seeing before me brought back those memories of you Jeff. I cried from my heart for that was where my tears began. My eyes were the vehicle that carried these tears from my body. I cried for this woman and I cried for myself. I cried for you and I cried because I wanted to. My heart felt compassion and my tears paid respect. I never thought about why some people cry and others do not. I never assumed that because someone doesn't cry that they are insensitive or unfeeling. Who am I to judge because they didn't react the same way that I did? Some people don't express their emotions by crying. They show their feelings in other ways. For some crying is a way of showing intimacy. For others crying is a way of showing one's feelings about important and meaningful things. Tears cleanse our eyes and help to sooth our aching hearts. Tears ease our pain and comfort those who suffer. Tears open up our minds and allow new thoughts and ideas to flow. To cry is to be human and to cry for someone else is to be humane.

Crying was always my way of responding to many emotional situations. Did I choose to cry or could I control my tears? Was I even capable of stopping myself before the first tears flowed from my eyes? The answer was NO, I could not. I was not an emotional faucet whose feelings could be turned on and off. The passion in my blood did not run hot and cold. I could not turn off my tears because the timing was inappropriate and/or inconvenient. When I cried in front of strangers or in public, I didn't worry about what people might have thought. There were times when perhaps I shouldn't have cried, because I had to protect the feelings of others. And there were times when I feared that if I started to cry, I might never be able to stop. I don't think I ever told you this, but I used to believe that my tears were like pearls. I was given so many at birth and they had to last a lifetime. I had to give them away wisely and carefully. I haven't given away all my pearls and I have many more to share.

You never wanted to make me cry but you could. You could make my eyes ache with tears so great that no amount of tissues or cloths could wipe them from my stained cheeks. During our marriage, my anger manifested itself through tears and the endless crying episodes drained both of us emotionally and mentally. My tears exhausted me. Days went by when crying was all that I did. I cried when we fought. I cried when you were going out on me. I cried when I heard about AIDS and for the next 10 years until you became ill. I cried as I remembered as a child how I ached when I was disappointed or when I didn't get my way. As a teenager, I expressed my frustrations and rage through tears, temper tantrums and hysterical outbursts. You knew from the moment we met how deeply I cared about you. And the thought that you would die from AIDS and the pain of watching you fight through the horror of this vicious disease opened up the floodgates of hell with tears that I never thought would ever stop. I cried myself to sleep for months after your death, because the last picture I held in my mind was your wasted body lying next to me. I cried for many reasons throughout the course of my life. I am thankful that I could and I've become more understanding of why I should.

The following story is about tears, fears, and a loving heart. It was a cool night and millions of stars were twinkling around a brilliant full moon. It was quiet at the center and most of the patients were asleep. There wasn't much for me to do, so I decided to go home early. As I was leaving, I noticed a small puddle outside this room. I looked up and saw water dripping from the ceiling. I reported it to maintenance, because I didn't want anyone to slip. I went back, wiped the water up, and placed a bucket under the leak. As I looked into the room, I noticed the curtain around the bed was open. I saw a young woman holding what I assumed to be her mother's hands. She was half leaning over the bed and swaying back and forth as if she was praying. I thought I should tell her about the leak outside the room. When I entered, I knew I had interrupted them. I felt uncomfortable and wanted to leave.

The daughter was having a terribly difficult time and her exhaustion was obvious. I said softly, "Hello. My name is Susan and I'm a volunteer. There is a water leak outside your room and I didn't want you to slip." I asked her if the woman was her mother. As she turned to answer me, I could see the tears streaming down her cheeks. She continued to sway back and forth, holding her mother's hands, weeping uncontrollably. I pulled out a handful of tissues and stuck them in her jacket pocket. I said, "The halls of hospice are shedding tears for you." "Yes, she said, perhaps they are crying for my mother." Her mother's eyes were closed and her tiny body looked lost in the bed covers. Tucked neatly under her left arm was a stuffed white teddy bear that said "Love." The woman's breathing was labored and her death was eminent. Both women had suffered the long-term effects of the disease. I placed my hand on her arm and apologized for interrupting them. I said, "It is very apparent how much you adore your mother. She is fortunate to have you for a daughter and that both of you have shared something very special together. It is beautiful to see such honest emotion and love."

The daughter stopped swaying and crying. She dried her eyes and said, "My mom was always there for me. I must be here for her now." However, it was what she said next that made this experience so powerful. She said, "I feel that I am being weak. I am not doing a very good job of being there for my mother now. I cry all the time. I feel that I am not being strong for her because I can not stop crying. She needs my comfort and support, but I am failing her. She never failed me. She was always there and she never cried. She made me feel safe. I am not doing a very good job now." Her comment caught me off guard. She saw her uncontrollable emotions as a sign of weakness and failure. She felt guilty because she was not in control of her emotions and she didn't want to fail her mother. Her grief and emotional exhaustion contributed to her feelings of inadequacy and guilt. Her perception of how she was handling the situation was entirely different than the way I perceived it. I saw her as strong, courageous, and loving. She adored her mother and the pain of watching her pass away was horrible. She was crying tears of sadness, love, and loss.

I wanted to tell her that I knew what she was feeling. There were times when I felt that I was failing you Jeff because I cried uncontrollably. The sadness and grief of saying good bye was excruciating. What could I say that might ease her sorrow? I said, "May I give you a hug? I could really use a hug." She half smiled and said, "Only if you let me take the box of tissues home." She let go of her mother's hands and wrapped her arms around me. I held her tightly against my chest and said, "You are crying because you love your mother and you are going to miss her. You are crying because you care about her and you are sad because she has suffered so much. You are crying because you are beautiful, passionate, and strong. You have seen your mother to the end and allowed her to pass with dignity and respect. You are everything a daughter should be and more." She started to relax and her tears gave way to a smile. My smile gave way to tears. She started to cry again and we were both pulling handfuls of tissues out of the box.

She said, "I hadn't thought of it that way. I always cried because I thought I was weak. I admired people who didn't cry. I'm not one of those." I said, "I've cried so much that I didn't think I'd ever be able to shed another tear. You've given your mother the greatest gift of all. She is very proud of you." She took her mother's hands again in hers and began telling her how much she loved her. I said good night and wished her the best. Her smile said it all as I walked out the door. She knew in her heart that she had done all the right things. Though our hug lasted only a few moments, its impact will remain with me forever. We were two strangers brought together by tissues and tears. Her love reinforced my belief that the only thing important in life is what you give to others. I've learned that there are many reasons for crying and I am very glad that I can. I hope that I'll never run out of pearls.

I'll say so long for a little while.

I love you.

Susan

Chapter 6

After His Tragic Year A Son Questions Whether He Will Ever Have Fun, Laugh, Or Feel Alive Again

"If I have to ask myself if I'm having fun, then I guess I'm not having any."

November 1998

Dear Jeff,

I don't know if I am afraid to die. Maybe the only way I'll know is when it happens. I wish I could hear your sweet voice and tender words of support and encouragement now. I am afraid and I need you to tell me that I'll be all right. Last week, a routine procedure indicated that I have a golf ball size mass protruding into my stomach. The doctors are trying to determine if it is benign or malignant. Can you believe it? I will know next week if my condition warrants surgery. If it does, it will be serious. It is important for me to start writing my feelings down. I've told many friends about my condition, but I have to express my fears and concerns on paper. My writing has always been my therapy and now I am even more thankful for it. My thoughts are frightening and I can not keep them locked up inside me. My words enable me to share this terribly difficult time with you. I've tried not to dwell on it and I am keeping busy. I know in my heart that I have the very best doctors taking care of me. I tell myself that there is nothing seriously wrong and that the doctors will not have to operate on me. However, I fear that they will and I am frightened.

For 25 years, you helped me through the roughest times in my life. No matter what the situation, you always knew what I needed and what to do. When I was ill you were the one I trusted to take care of me. You babied me when I needed to be babied and you nursed me when I needed to be nursed. You were always supposed to be there for me. I need you more than ever. I need my best friend's positive attitude and strength. I need you to give me hope and send me a sign telling me that I will be all right. You were the one who taught me to live each day as if it were the last. From the time we met you always said, "Life was too short and time was so precious. Don't look back and never waste time." How did you live with the possibility that you might become HIV positive? It had to have been horrible knowing that every time you had something physically wrong, the first thing that came into your mind was the thought of AIDS. Whenever you were ill with a cold, an ache or a pain, I worried and feared for your life. When you were diagnosed with pneumonia, it was your courage and strength that inspired me and thus enabling me to go on. You kept me going when I wanted to give up. After you passed away, there were times when I didn't think that I would ever feel alive again.

I was in shock, numb, and raw. I was dead inside with an empty heart beating, grieving, and crying out in despair. I felt nothing yet I was aware of everything. I tried to focus on the beautiful memories of the life we once shared, but the torment I felt was unbearable. It hurt too badly to think about the past. Would I ever laugh again I asked myself? Would I every feel happiness and joy? How could I ever love life again when I hated it so much? How could I have been born into this cruel and unjust world? I believed that heartache and sorrow would be a permanent part of my life. And last night at the care center I met a man who was asking himself the same questions I once had asked. As I listened to his story, I understood all too well his feelings of helplessness and despair.

It was a cold autumn night and I didn't want to go out. However, I knew that I'd feel better once I was there. Feeling needed by helping other people always took my mind off of my own problems. When I saw the patients and their families coping with the most difficult times of their lives, their strength and courage renewed my faith and gave me hope. And the never-ending positive attitude and support from my friends always helped to lessen my fears. I checked in at the center, got the ice bucket and started delivering water to the patients. I knocked on the door several times, but no one answered. I was going to leave when I heard a man's voice telling me to come in. I walked over to the bed and said, "Hello, my name is Susan. I'm a volunteer. May I get you something?" He didn't respond to my question and stared at me as if he hadn't heard a word I'd said. I repeated myself stating that I would be on call tonight if he needed anything. He had a dazed, trance like look on his face that was void of any emotion. He appeared unaware of everything and I wasn't sure what to do next.

I said, "Would you like to have a cup of coffee with me? It's good to get up take a break. If you want to talk, I'd like to listen." He said, "I don't know what I want and I don't know how I should feel. I am empty inside but I am not the one who is dying." I said, "Please come and have just one cup with me." "Okay, he said, my mother will be all right for a little while." We poured ourselves the coffee and sat down. He was exhausted almost too tired to think or speak. He didn't know what to do next. I felt so sorry for him. It was an awkward time for me because I didn't know what to say and I didn't want to upset him even more. He continued to stare into the coffee cup, twirling his spoon around and around. I said, "Your mother isn't in any pain and is comfortable. Hospice is about the quality of life and she is having that here. I think that you've been a very loving and devoted son." He said, "It's been the year from hell. My dad passed away 13 months ago from a massive heart attack. He died in my arms. I moved back home to help my mother out. Now, one year later, I must say goodbye to her. I don't think that I'll ever feel good again. I can't remember ever having fun or laughing. I don't feel anything but sorrow and I am trapped in a life I wish never existed." He finished his coffee and excused himself. He went back to check on his mother. I said that I would be here for a couple of hours and would say goodnight before I left.

About an hour later, he came over and tapped me on the shoulder. He said, "Mom is all right. Could I tell you what's happened to me this past year? I don't know why I'm being tested this way. Why have these things happened?" I said, "I don't know why anything happens anymore and I stopped asking the why question a long time ago. I'd like to hear your story. Maybe talking about it will make you feel better." He said, "Dad had a massive heart attack and died instantly. About 3 months later, my wife of 22 years divorced me and ran off with my best friend. Three months after that, the company I worked for filed Chapter 11 and I got laid off. My mother developed pancreatic cancer and now I'm taking care of her." He blurted all this information out in two sentences. He never paused or hesitated. He was like an actor reading lines from a script written especially for him. But, it was what happened next that surprised me. Once he heard his own story, he started to laugh. He was laughing so hard that I started to laugh along with him. We couldn't control ourselves.

He finally said, "I needed that. I don't remember the last time I felt good, or laughed, or even felt alive. As I was telling you about the past year, it sounded so ridiculous, that I didn't think I was talking about myself. All I cared about was my mother. I wanted her to be comfortable and out of pain. If I'm being tested, I think that I've failed. I know I used to be happy. I had energy and "spunk" as my parents called it. Where did all the laughter go? Has it all been replaced with pain and sorrow? Do you think that I will ever feel alive again or be happy? I don't have any energy and I'm not motivated about doing anything. I'm not dead but I feel that way inside." I said, "My husband died 4 years ago after a long illness. I understand everything you have said to me. I've felt the same way and questioned the same things. I was so emotionally drained and exhausted that I couldn't think any more. As I watched my life play out in total chaos, I had no plan for the future. I didn't want a future. Then slowly, one day at a time, the pain and sadness got a little easier to bear. One day I smiled and I meant it. I woke up one morning because I wanted to. One day I started to feel all right again and you will, too. You will be stronger than you were before because you have given your mother the greatest gift of all. You were there at her side when she needed you the most. You gave of yourself and you gave from the heart." We talked a little longer then said good night. He went back to be with his mother and I went home. His mother passed away during the night with her son at her side.

When I got home I couldn't get his words out of my mind. Was it hypocritical of me to try and reassure him that one day he would be all right, when I was frightened to death about my own condition? Maybe the answer was yes or maybe it was no. I told him how I felt about what he was going through. He cared deeply for his mother and did what he had to do when it truly mattered. Then I flashed back and realized that this story reminded me of a test you gave to a group of students at one of your psychology seminars. You asked everyone in the class to list in order of importance what needs they felt were their strongest. The needs mentioned were fun, freedom, power, and recognition. There were many questions and they had different scenarios and outcomes. There weren't any right or wrongs answers or points to score. It was just a generic evaluation that caused one to reflect on what they felt were their priorities in life. Then we thought that it would be fun to take the test ourselves. When it was over, both of us listed freedom first, fun second, recognition third, and power last. Oh, how we laughed for days about how freedom and fun were our best qualities and also our worst. Yes, we required a lot of both. I miss our fun, the laughter, and I will always miss us.

I'll say so long for a little while.

I love you.

Susan

Chapter 7

As A Wife Sat Reading Her Bible Praying For Peace, She Was Caught In A Catch 22 For She Was Cherishing Every Moment While Wishing This Time Was Over

"Is there a difference between feeling peaceful and being at peace?"

December 1998,

Dear Jeff,

Letting go and relinquishing control over the things that I have no control over has been a long and complicated process for me and learning to love and unconditionally accept myself still remains a constant challenge. This task is made even more difficult because I am dealing with a steadfast adversary who will never go away. Of this I am certain for the enemy I must constantly battle is myself. I can still hear you saying to me, "Susan, you are so restless. You make things much more difficult than they have to be. It will be very hard for you to find peace and harmony in your life." Jeff, you knew me so well and your honest opinions were always correct. However, the more I continue to find out about myself, the less afraid of the future I am becoming. Perhaps it's my pursuit for knowledge and insight that will ultimately bring me the peace that I've been searching for. I know that I feel the greatest comfort when I accept the fact that wherever I am in my life that is where I am supposed to be. Though these times are less frequent, I continue to ride an emotional roller coaster, pushing and challenging myself while searching for the perfect balance between peace of heart and peace of mind. When I am frightened, under pressure, or feeling stressed out, I question if there is such a thing as inner peace. It's during these times of uncertainty and instability that I find it difficult to remain positive and optimistic and when I could use your words of encouragement the most.

Last night, I met a woman who was searching for her own kind of peace. As she faced the loss of her husband, her feelings of guilt and unrest made her question if she had done the right thing. Again tonight, I found myself understanding why she felt this way because it was just 4 years ago when I had to deal with the very same issue. As I checked into the care center it was a very busy night. All the beds were occupied and there were family members everywhere. With this many people around, I felt that it was important to go into the rooms and introduce myself. As I knocked on the door, a woman's voice said, "Please come in." The table lamp was on low and a large white candle cast a beautiful soft glow throughout the room. There was a full moon shining through the open shutters and the room looked peaceful and serene. I barely noticed the slender body sitting in the moonlight next to the bed. As I came closer, she smiled and said, "Hello. I haven't seen you before, have I?" "No, I said. My name is Susan and I'm the volunteer on call tonight. Is there anything I can get for you?" "Oh yes, she said, I could use some peace in my heart right now." I responded, "That would be a blessing because you probably haven't felt any peace in your life for a long time. Would you like a little company?" "Yes, she said, that would be nice." She asked me to turn the lights up to make the room a little brighter. Her voice was kind and sincere, but it was her gentle manner that I was immediately drawn to.

She was wearing a Jewish star set in blue Lapis around her neck. There was a book resting in her lap entitled, The Book of Rachel. I said, "I assume from the book you are reading and the Star of David around your neck, that you are Jewish." "Oh yes, she said, I was born in Germany but my family left when I was very young." I said, "My grandparents were from Poland and Russia and I was raised in a strict Orthodox Jewish home. I've made some very different choices, however, along the way." She smiled and said, "Me too. My personal beliefs in God came later on in life. During the past few years, my faith has been tested and at the moment I don't know what I believe in. My husband slipped into a coma this morning and I can't bear to watch him suffer any longer. I still reach over and touch his arm and hold his hand, but he is not with me now." We sat in silence staring at the man breathing softly in his bed. She continued, "This is a sadness and pain I have never known. There is no peace in my heart or in my life. I want him to wake up and talk to me. I want to take him home again and have him near me. Please tell him to wake up and talk to me." Her eyes welled up and in a soft heartbroken voice she said, "I still want him with me, yet I want his suffering to end and for his pain to go away. I want this to be over with, but I want him in my life. Isn't that a terrible way to feel?" Her words were powerful and they brought back images and the same feelings I had during the final days of your life.

She started to fidget with a handkerchief that was tucked under her watch. As the tears rolled down her cheeks, I jumped up and grabbed the box of tissues from the nightstand. I said, "Forget the hankie! Take the whole box. This is definitely a time for the whole box." Her smile told me that it was all right for me to share my personal feelings with her. I said, "I understand the way you feel, because I felt the same way when my husband had died. It is a very common issue when dealing with a long-term illness." She said, "I'm 77 years old and my husband is 82. He's had Parkinson's disease for many years and has been confined to the house for the last 2. We've been partners for 55 years. I was so content with being his wife. I never wanted anything else. My two children live in New York and visit regularly, but I've always been a wife first. I am a mother, but I loved being his wife. There wasn't anything left for us to do but to be together. I made our meals everyday though he didn't always have an appetite. We watched TV and just sat holding hands. I pushed our twin beds together because I wanted to fall asleep feeling him next to me. I was his caregiver and I wanted him with me as long as possible. I didn't care about the conditions or the circumstances. But, his pain was continuous and I had to bring him here. Now, I just want him to wake up one more time to say I love you and goodbye."

She asked me why I got involved with hospice. I said, "My husband suffered with a long term illness and hospice helped me to get through the last few weeks of his life. When I come here, I feel like I am doing something worthwhile with the experiences I've been through. I understand what you are telling me, because I felt the same way. I wanted him in my life forever, no matter what the circumstances. But, there wasn't any quality of life for either of us. I desperately wanted him to be with me, but I wanted it to be over with, too. It was a horrible feeling to have." She took her Star of David in her hands and said, "I know that one day I will feel some peace and stability again in my life, but it will take a long time. Peace of mind and peace of heart are what I pray for now. It's funny, but as difficult as the past few years have been, I can't remember any of the bad times we shared. I've loved every minute of it." We hugged each other and said good night. When I got home, I couldn't stop thinking about this remarkable woman and the love she had for her husband. She helped me to remember the time in my life when you were just hanging on, but I wanted to hear every breath, to touch your hand, and to feel your skin just a little longer. There was always going to be just one more time. I wanted my life to go on and though this time was excruciating, I didn't want it to end. We were going to grow old together and I didn't care what compromises I had to make. I didn't care if we went out, if you ate, or even if you were in the room with me. I just wanted you to stay with me a little bit longer. Yes, I wanted your suffering to end and for you to be at peace. So I prayed for peace for the both of us.

As mentioned so many times, it had been through my writing that I had discovered what being true to myself had meant and most of the times those became the greatest most satisfyingly peaceful times I'd ever known. I had found inner peace when I've recognized the fact that the decisions I'd made had been my own, no matter how difficult they might have been. I'd also found both peace of mind and peace of heart when I wrote these story letters to you. It was challenging to try to convey other people's lives and their issues through unspoken thoughts and written words. But finally, I'd found tremendous peace in my heart as I assisted others going through the most difficult times of their life. Perhaps true inner peace is but a temporary feeling, but it's a feeling that can last forever. I will continue searching for that permanent state of unconditional acceptance of myself, but the most important thing that I hope to achieve in the end is that I did my life my way.

The decisions I'd made were always the right ones and I don't ever want to look back and have any regrets. I wanted you in my life forever and never wanted to say good-bye, but I am thankful that you were finally at peace. It was only through my own intense scrutiny and self-exploration that this new found self-awareness and peace in my life had begun. Finding inner peace for myself had been both frightening and challenging, but I'd discovered that I did enjoy the feelings of being both powerless and powerful. As I have become more peaceful with myself, I have become more at peace with others. We never talked about what peace meant to us, but I hope that you had great peace of heart and peace of mind in your life. I am finding it much more peaceful as I continue on my journey and I thank you for helping me along the way.

I'll say so long for a little while.

I love you.

Susan

Chapter 8

A Wife Questions How She Will Start Over After Her Husband's Death and What She Will Do With Her Time Alone

"I will take the time to let the time take care of me."

January 17th, 1999

Dear Jeff,

According to Webster's dictionary, commitment means to pledge, to obligate oneself, or to promise. For me, commitment also meant responsibility. When I said the words, "until death do us part" on January 11th, 1969, I made my commitment to you. That unconditional promise continued to remain the most important aspect of my relationship with you. There were many times during our 25-year marriage when I didn't like you, but I never stopped loving you. Our relationship was turbulent and our quarrels over your homosexuality nearly destroyed me, but no matter how many times I tried to leave you, I never could. If our marriage were to end, you would've had to be the one who left for with you my life was so fulfilling and incredibly rewarding. It was a rollercoaster ride that I never wanted to get off of. There was passion and it was exciting. My world revolved around our home and your career. I was determined to make our relationship work because we were worth fighting for.

After you died, I didn't know if I would be able to go on. For weeks, I didn't want to get out of bed. I'd pull the covers over my head and clutch your pillow to my chest. I pushed myself to leave the house and when it was time to come home, I'd ask myself what did I have to come home to? It was an effort to do the things I once enjoyed doing and it was painful to remember the wonderful times we shared. This new life I had to make for myself felt awkward and uncomfortable. I was thrown into situations that were painfully difficult to accept and I was forced to make endless adjustments and compromises to issues and circumstances I didn't understand. I was not prepared to be alone nor did I want to be. My life had been drastically changed and I had to change and adjust to it. This transition from married life to widowhood took a very long time. I went forwards and backwards, yet I felt like I was going no where.

However, one day what I thought to be an impossible task had been accomplished. I had succeeded in making a new life for myself.

Last week at the care center, I met a woman who would soon be widowed. Her concerns and the issues she addressed about her uncertain future were the same ones that I had to deal with after you died. This remarkable woman and her passionate story seemed even more appropriate at this time, because she and I met on the night of January 11th. Tonight would have been our 30th wedding anniversary. As I went on shift and checked in that night, it was extremely quiet. Most of the patients were sleeping and there were only a few visitors around. I noticed a magnificent looking woman standing in the doorway of the room. I couldn't stop starring at her, and though I tried not to be obvious, I couldn't help myself. She was tall, stunning, and stately with a flawless complexion the color of a porcelain doll. Her grayish-white hair was cut in a Dutch-boy style that framed her finely chiseled features.

I had no idea how old she was, but she radiated a natural beauty that made her look comfortable with herself no matter what her age might be. She looked like she belonged on the cover of a magazine. I walked towards her and said, "Hello, my name is Susan and I am a volunteer here tonight. If I can get you anything, please don't hesitate to ask." She looked at me and said, "How can you have such a beautiful tan in the middle of January? I always loved the sun but I was told to avoid it at all costs. Well, I guess that says a lot for my Mayflower heritage." I said, "I think that you are absolutely breathtaking. I shall call us a mutual admiration society of two." We smiled at each other as if we had shared something very special. She said, "I like that. I think that most people always want to look like someone else. Right now, I'd like to be someone else."

I asked her if she had ever modeled. She laughed and said, "I did that for many years. Is it that obvious?" "Oh yes, I said. As soon as I saw you that was the first thing I thought of." She responded, "That's how I met my husband 35 years ago. We made the perfect 10. I was always so tall and thin and he was one big hunk of a man." She beamed as she spoke about him. I asked her if she would like some company and she said, "Yes." As we went into the room she closed the door. She said, "I like my privacy. I brought my husband in for pain management two days ago. Even though he's heavily medicated, we still manage to communicate with each other." I watched how they interacted. She was absolutely devoted and emanated love for him while his eyes followed her every movement responding to her voice. Everything she did reminded me of the time when you and I were going through the very same thing.

I found myself getting emotionally caught up in their relationship and I almost had to leave the room. She said, "Why do you volunteer for hospice?" I responded, "My husband died 4 years ago and hospice came into our home and helped me care for him." She said, "My husband had a boating accident 34 years ago that left him disabled. Now he has Hodgkin's disease and since he was such a large man, I needed to bring him here. I wanted him to remain at home, but it was too difficult." She looked at me with her gorgeous blue eyes and said, "What am I going to do with all my time when this is over? I made a commitment to him 34 years ago and even when he was seriously hurt, I was the one who took care of him. What will I do with my time?"

She continued, "When I took my wedding vows and said "I do," I said it with my heart. No matter what ever happened, there would be no turning back. I would love him forever, would never have left him, and I would never have given up on us. That's what I believe and that's what I did." Her statement brought tears to my eyes, because I felt the same way. We both believed in the power of the word "commitment." Looking at this beautiful woman I could never have imagined that she had ever known anything but fun or had a care in the world. However, as she continued, her story was just the opposite. She said, "I met my husband while I was modeling. We fell in love immediately. We had a son who developed leukemia when he was 17 years old. He died 6 months later. We tried everything but it happened so quickly. Nothing the doctors did would work. It was the most painful experience we could have ever imagined. We dealt with it together and somehow it made us stronger. Three years later my husband was in a serious boating accident and for weeks I didn't know if he would live or die. He's been confined to a wheelchair ever since. My life was thrown into turmoil when our son died and then I had to deal with this. But, my husband needed me and I was determined to make it the best it could be. Now, all I can think about is how difficult it will be without him."

I went to get her a cup of coffee and when I came back, his hearing aid had fallen out. The oxygen tubing in his nose had gotten tangled under the sheets and twisted around his hospital gown. He was miserable and fidgeting with everything. She couldn't get the hearing aid back in his ear and asked me if I would help. We were so clumsy and though we tried desperately not to laugh, it was very comical. I said, "I feel like one of the three stooges. I don't think that 6 hands are better than two right about now." An aide came into the room and when we looked at her, we burst out laughing. It took us 15 minutes to finally get his little hearing aid back into place and undo the twisted tube. When we stepped outside she said, "Thank you. I hadn't had a good laugh in a long time. What am I going to do with all my time afterwards? There are no children or grandchildren to fuss over and I've spent most of my time caring for him. I'm going to need a lot of time to adjust to my "new skin." I used to play golf, liked to paint, and traveled when I was modeling. I'm not going to be able to make any long term plans and I'll just have to try and take each day as it comes." I said, "Take the time to let the time take care of you. Good night beautiful lady."

I came by several times during the week to visit with her. We always giggled over the little project that brought us together. I never gave her any advice nor did she ask for any. We were two women talking about similar feelings and issues. I told her how I dealt with my time after you died and some of the situations I had to face. We understood each other and our time together helped us both. I thought about this woman a lot during the week. I was in awe of her character, strength, determination, loyalty, but mostly it was her positive attitude about life that I admired. And our conversation brought up many of the same issues that I had to deal with after you passed away. We never had any children, my life revolved around you, and I was going to have a lot of time afterwards, too.

I questioned what I was going to do with the empty spaces and the voids in my life, but I didn't rush into anything too quickly. I had many options afterwards but I didn't feel comfortable with any of them. I was raw and numb and knew that I had to take one day at a time. Time can work both for you and against you. I chose to take a lot of time to heal, to deal with my loss and grief, and hoped that in time I would gain the strength to go on. When I felt that I needed support and the help from family and friends, I asked for it. But, my new life and the future ahead were for me to determine and it was up to me to see myself through it. I know that having a positive attitude also helped. Slowly I went back to the things I had previously enjoyed but I also allowed new interests and people into my life. This lady was going to be all right one day because she was going to "take the time to let the time take care of her."

I'll say so long for a little while.

I love you and HAPPY BIRTHDAY.

Susan

Chapter 9

When A Life Threatening Illness Tested The Power Of His Faith He Envied Those Who Truly Believed in God

"Can the human touch be as powerful as a drug?"

February 14th, 1999

Dear Jeff,

I never told you this, but I envied the fact that your belief in God and your spirituality was always stronger than mine. However, I am proud to say that we never once had a disagreement or argument over our religious beliefs? It was very comforting to know that religious matters never presented any problems to us because we came from similar backgrounds. We were raised by parents who believed in God and who took the time to teach us about basic Jewish values and traditions. We were married in your synagogue by the same rabbi who performed your Bar Mitzvah. When you said that you wished to be cremated, I was thankful that this was not a religious issue that we had to deal with.

We both believed in a higher power and shared a proud and honored Jewish heritage.

It was our solid foundation in Judaism that gave us the valuable information and the skills we needed to help get us through the most difficult times. During our 25-year marriage, there were two occasions when my faith and belief in God was seriously tested. Once was in Houston in 1975. My world was collapsing around me. Your homosexual affairs were destroying me. Our marriage was in chaos and my life was out of control. It was my belief and trust then in God that prevented me from killing myself. The second one was in Boca Raton, in 1992 when you were diagnosed with AIDS. It was that diagnosis and your illness that made me question if there was a God at all. I tried to deny my faith and I hated a God who could be so cruel, but I continued to do what I always did. I put myself back into God's hands and asked for the strength to help me to get through.

A few weeks ago at the care center, I met a man who was questioning his religious beliefs. He shared with me his feelings of guilt because he didn't believe as strongly as he thought he should. His story was important to me because this issue was one that I still continue to struggle with at this time. This story starts as I went on shift that one incredible night. I was never able to predict whether the center would be quiet, busy, or at times empty without patients and/or visitors. Tonight, however, it was exceptionally busy and the patient call buttons were going off in every room. As quickly as the lights were turned off and the matter attended to, another room would light up with the steady beeps sounding throughout the halls. When I went to respond to this particular call, the man I saw in bed could only be described as "beautiful." He had a peaches and cream complexion with a youthful appearance that made him look like he was ready to play 18 rounds of golf. I turned off his button and said, "Hi. I'm Susan a volunteer. May I help you with something?" I saw that his hands and legs were trembling, but his eyes told me what I needed to know. I said, "I will tell your nurse that you are in pain."

He said, "Would you please come back? I don't want to be alone." I took his trembling hands in mine and said, "You can count on it. I'll stay with you as long as you want." I told his nurse and she said that she would be in immediately. When I got back to the room, his tremors had gotten worse. I lowered the bed rail and held his hands. I began messaging them trying to take his mind off the pain. We never spoke. A few minutes later his nurse came with his medication. He said to her, "My tremors have stopped and my pain is not so severe. I think this lady has a miracle touch." I said, "I just helped him focus on something else till you arrived." After she gave him his medication he said, "Would you stay with me a while?" "Oh, yes, I said, I would like that."

I pulled a chair up close to the bed and waited for the medication to take effect. Within minutes his pain was gone and his body relaxed. He said, "I envy people who truly believe with all their heart in God. I never really questioned or doubted that there was a God, but I don't feel the peace and comfort that so many people do." I said, "You aren't the only one." His warm smile indicated that we had shared something very personal. He said, "I like the Jewish Star around your neck. I'm Jewish, too." I said, "Your name and your appearance gave it away. We are kindred spirits." He said, "I'm 66 years old and I've had prostate cancer for 10 years. I'm here to get the pain under control. The doctors can't do anything else for me." I said, "You look like the picture of health. I would never have known that you were ill."

He said, "I accept the fact that I am dying, but do you know what I am feeling guilty about? It troubles me that I don't believe in my faith as much as I think I should. I was raised in a Jewish home with Jewish values and traditions. I was always proud of my religious background but something was missing. It wasn't enough for me to conduct my life as a Jew. The rewards weren't enough. I started to honestly question my belief in God when my cancer was diagnosed. Why God should I have to suffer like this had become my mantra. It's my fear of the pain and the uncertainty of the disease's progression that causes me to doubt my beliefs the most. I seem to believe more in God when I am pain free and have some quality in my life. Have you heard this before?" I said, "Yes, many times. I'm dealing with the same issues but for different reasons. My life is in a transition and I am questioning how strong my faith and beliefs are." He started to get sleepy and asked me if I would come again tomorrow. I said, "I look forward to it." He responded, "Thank you for understanding."

When I arrived the next day he said, "I've had my medication and am very comfortable." I gave him a hug, put down the side rail, and pulled up a chair. I said, "I'm all yours. What should we talk about?" He said, "Do you think it's normal to question your faith and belief in God at different times in your life?" I said, "Of course. In fact, I got so depressed for a while when we lived in Houston that I actually joined a synagogue. I had to find something to believe in or someone to give me the strength and courage to get through. If I hadn't questioned my beliefs, I would have ended my marriage or perhaps taken my own life. In time, this decision proved to be one of the best things I had ever done. It helped me to understand why I was so committed to my marriage and it contributed to a higher level of understanding and acceptance of the world around me." Then he asked me if I had a job. "Oh no, I said. I'm a professional volunteer and a writer.

I love helping people and writing human-interest stories. After my husband died, I had to do something with the information and experiences I'd been through. Volunteering and writing seemed to be the things that gave me the most happiness." He got very excited and reached into his night table. He took out a spiral notebook and said, "This is wonderful. I'm writing a book of stories to my family and friends. I want them to know just how much their love, devotion, and friendship have meant to me all these years. This book will be something that they can share together afterwards. I wish I had done it sooner." He started reading from his journal. His short simple sentences conveyed words of powerful emotions and passionate feelings to those he cared about. I told him I kept daily journals when you were ill and it was the writing that gave me the strength to go on. I said, "Why don't you dictate your stories to me. I can help you write your memoirs."

By the end of the evening we'd completed a wonderful story about his teenage years growing up in New York. He fell asleep as I read it back to him. I left a note on his journal stating that his secretary would be back tomorrow. When I got there the next day, a dozen people were visiting him. They were having a birthday party for his wife. His beautiful face lit up when he saw me. "Hi, secretary," he said. "Hi, memoir man, I responded." We giggled at each other. But, what surprised me was when everyone yelled, "Hi, secretary." He had told everyone about what we were doing. His wife came over, hugged me and said, "He hasn't been this excited about anything in a long time. Thank you." I said, "I think we're going for a Pulitzer." His wife mentioned that the hospice rabbi brought by a flyer about a Sabbath Service to be aired on a local radio station tonight at 7:30.

She thought that it would be beneficial for him to listen to it. His family was about to leave and since I hadn't been to a Friday night Sabbath Service for a long time, I asked if I could stay and listen with him. I had a tape recorder and a blank cassette in my hospice bag and thought that it would be a good idea to tape the service. He looked surprised when he saw the recorder. I said, "I'm not into lipstick or hairbrushes." He laughed and said, "You're a true writer." I brought him his dinner tray, found the station, and we started listening to the service. Though he dozed occasionally, he stayed awake for the rabbi's sermon. He said, "I think this is exactly what I needed now. I am glad you taped it because I want to listen to it again with my wife." I kissed his forehead and said "Good Shabbas. Tonight helped both of us to believe that there was a higher power that would help us through the difficult times." He said, "Thank you for everything. There will always be a special place in my heart for you."

This courageous man dealt with an issue that many people have addressed while going through adversity and troubling times. I visited with him during the next few weeks and though we continued our writing, we never talked again about his beliefs or if his faith in God was any stronger. I know that our time together made a significant difference to both of us. Sharing his concerns made me think about my belief in God, my Jewish heritage, and the power of that faith to believe in myself. I never thought that he would have such a profound effect on me. I know that I still have questions and doubts about how strongly and steadfastly I do believe, but I don't have any guilt about it now. This man helped me to understand that I have the right to challenge the strength of my beliefs. If I continue to ask the right questions, I will get the right answers. For now, it is comforting just to know that I do believe in a higher power and that I will make it through the years that follow. One day I hope that no matter how difficult the situation or how much I am tested, that I will not falter in my beliefs. I must trust in the fact that there is always an end in sight and that I have the power to believe or not to believe. You once said, "Sometimes the rewards in life aren't what we expect, but they are what they are supposed to be." You were my greatest reward and I'll never stop believing in you."

I'll say so long for a little while.

I love you and Happy Valentine's Day.

Susan

Chapter 10

As Her Father Was Dying She Said That It Reminded Her Of Her Child At Birth-It Was A Complete 360 And The Totality Of The Cycle Of Life

"You became the child I never had but you were still the man I loved."

March 1999

Dear Jeff,

If I hadn't gotten pregnant, we would never have been married. If abortion had been legalized in 1969, we would have chosen to do that instead. After my miscarriage, we could have had our marriage annulled. That would have been the easiest thing to do. So why didn't we call it quits? Why? Why? Why? It was because we cared about each other. We were best friends and we wanted to try and make our marriage work and we continued trying for 25 years. I am thankful that we didn't have any children. We never wanted them and we couldn't find any reasons why we should. We were thrown together in a marriage that neither of us wanted and we were not prepared for the personal sacrifices it entailed. We were so young and too naïve. We had our own issues to deal with. We were too selfish to have children. They would have interfered with our plans. We could never live a conventional lifestyle. We liked our freedom and independence too much to give it up and your homosexuality had become a part of our marriage. You weren't going to change and I had to accept it or leave you. How could we assume the responsibility of a child? As time went by, we continued to set goals and prioritize what it was that we both wanted out of our marriage. We always agreed on one thing. Our lifestyle would not have been conducive for raising children.

Last night I met a woman who expressed some powerful thoughts about birth, death, and the similarities between them both. She called it the "360-degree completion of life." Her story brought back memories of the child we lost and the cruel disease that took your life, but it helped me to understand what the word "completion" really meant. Oh, how these people and their stories have taken me back and yet forward at the same time. That's what sometimes gets to me. I never know what to expect when I go there and it's the anticipation that I look forward to. Tonight would prove to be no different and yet very different than any other night.

It was unusually still when I arrived and it felt strange. Even the nurse's station was quiet and the aids were gathered together softly speaking in the hallway. It was 6:00 PM and there should have been people milling around having coffee or speaking with the staff. There were very few patients and it seemed like there was nothing to do. I got my cart, water pitcher, and ice and was drawn into a corner room. Before I knocked on the door, I hesitated because I felt like someone or something was holding me back keeping me stationary unable to move. After what seemed like minutes, I proceeded to knock on the door, but the woman inside did not hear me. She was staring out into the courtyard with her back towards me.

I came closer and said, "Hello." She jumped and said, "Oh, you startled me." I responded, "I'm sorry to have frightened you. I'm Susan, a volunteer. I knocked but you seemed to be deep in thought. You probably have a million things going through your mind." She said, "I keep thinking about how energetic my father used to be. He was bigger than life. My 3 children adored their grandfather. They never slept the night before his visits because they were so excited. They eagerly awaited his humorous and adventurous stories. He would tell the same ones over and over again, but the kids never left his side. When I had my first child my father wouldn't leave the room. He stood over the crib and told stories to his grandchild. He wouldn't stop. He was a storyteller and felt that children were the best audience to tell his stories to because they couldn't talk back or get up and leave. That was my dad. His energy was endless and his devotion to his family was his greatest pleasure. It was just a few weeks ago that he looked like my father, but sadly now he does not.

As I stare at him he looks like my son when he was born. I can't believe how much birth and death have in common. They are so frighteningly similar. It's the 360-degree completion of the life cycle." Her words hit me hard like a sledgehammer whacking me on the side of the head. I gasped losing my breath for a moment, but I don't think she was aware of the uncomfortable feeling I was experiencing. I felt like my skin was on fire and a part of me wanted to leave the room. Why? Why did this woman and what she had just said have such an impact on my spirit? Why? Because that was how I felt as I watched you slowly waste away. You were an adult who had become a child. I couldn't find the words to tell her that I understood her feelings but instinctively I reached out and took her hand. She said, "You've heard that before haven't you?" "Oh yes, I said, it's a feeling that many people have shared with me. I felt the same way five years ago as I watched my husband die. I don't think that you have to have a child to see the similarities between infancy and the final stages of the dying process. But, what was it in particular that made you feel that way and say what you did?"

She walked closer to the bed and messaged her father's hands. She said, "He looks so helpless and innocent. He has to be watched over and protected. His needs have to be taken care of by others and he requires so much attention and care." I said, "Would you like to step outside and have a cup of coffee with me?" "Yes, she said, that would be nice. I can't believe I feel this way, but it certainly puts dying into perspective." She kissed him on the forehead and straightened up his blanket. She said, "I'll be back in a little while dad. I love you." We poured ourselves some coffee and sat down. She reached for the tissues and grabbed a handful. She said, "Hot coffee and tissues 24 hours a day and at a time like this, what more can anyone ask for?" "How about a good night's sleep," I said. She smiled and said, "For me to be able to share this final chapter of his life with him will be the greatest gift I could have given him. Being with my father at his moment of death will give me a feeling of completion. My journey with him will be over for now." I said, "When my husband died, I felt like I had completed a journey with him. As much as I wanted him in my life, a part of me felt as if I had done something whole and final. No loose ends to tie up. Nothing left undone or unsaid."

We paused for a moment, took a sip of coffee, and then I said, "I was with him when he died and it was that 360-degree completion that enabled me to go on. I helped him through the most difficult time in his life and he trusted me every step of the way. He knew that I would have done whatever he wanted me to do to. It can't be explained. It was something that you must experience yourself. It was that feeling of having accomplished something so overwhelmingly powerful that it made me more aware of my surroundings, my future, and myself. I knew that I wouldn't have any guilt or regrets afterwards. One day I would be able to go forward feeling stronger and more confident because I had made it through this tragic time. There would be an incredible feeling of accomplishment that would be gained having gone through such adversity." She took my hand and said, "Completion is a very important thing to have. I feel like I made a full circle with my Dad. I see him now in his bed dying yet I see him as my child at birth. I am watching him go through this final passage and I am so thankful that I could be there with him. I am so fortunate to have done it all with him and said it all before this time. I was not there when my mother passed away and somehow I feel like I failed her because I wasn't there. I didn't know that she had died until she had passed and though I was able to attend the funeral and be with my family afterwards, it was not the same thing as being with her."

She wanted to get back to the room. I asked if she would like some company. She said simply, "Yes." She walked over to her father and over and over again she said, "Dad, I love you. I love you." She sat down and gently continued to message his hands and arms. She said, "I've lived in the same house for 26 years until I got married. It's the only home my parents ever owned. My husband and I live close by and there is only one teenage son left at home. That makes it easier for me to stay here with dad. My younger sister is not coping well with any of this. She lives in New York and has a career and family to contend with. She can't come here now and has her own issues to deal with. She was closer with my mother and I was closer with my dad. I love my sister, but we never had that close relationship I would have liked. After mom died from a heart attack, Dad came down to Florida for a visit and he never left." Her comment made me laugh. I said, "That's another issue I've heard about. Maybe several hundred times before." She smiled and said, "I loved his honesty, his enthusiasm, and his patience. He was such a gentle and kind soul. You couldn't help but love him. I get my positive attitude and love for beauty and nature from my father." She reached for the tissues, grabbed another handful, and thrust the box at me. If two strangers ever bonded, it was tonight over some heartfelt and honest conversation.

She continued, "You understand what I am saying, don't you?" "Yes, I said. Everything that you have said is true. That's one of the reasons I volunteer for hospice. I understand what many people are feeling. When you spoke about the completion of the cycle, that's the way I felt." Again she said, "He really does remind me of my child when he was in the crib. I should be telling him stories. Yes, birth and death have a lot in common. He is curled up in a fetal position. He is wearing a diaper. His needs are very simple but they are still important. He has become dependent on everyone else. I never knew that I could feel this way." She leaned over and whispered in his ear, "I love you, Dad. I know in my heart that everything we had together as a father and daughter was so honest and good. We were friends. We were best friends. You were my best friend, Dad." And my father would always say, "Thank you for being my child." Dad this is my way of saying back to you, "Thank you for allowing me to be your daughter and for having such trust in me throughout my life." I said, "You will get stronger and go forward with peace in your heart because of what you are going through. You are definitely your father's daughter. Good night."

On the way home, I starting thinking about my 30th birthday and the hospital party you gave for me. You asked me what I wanted for my birthday. I said, "I don't want any children but I do want my tubes tied. We know that we don't want children so what are we waiting for? You can throw me a tubal ligation cutting ceremony." And you did. You gave me a party and invited our friends to the hospital. It was wonderful. I wonder what our life would have been like if we'd had children. I know that we would have been good parents. I'm sorry for the hundreds of times that I treated you like a child and failed to deal with you like an adult. I think that my "taking care of you issue" got too intense at times. I only wanted to be your wife and best friend. I didn't know where our friendship was going, but I knew that it would continue. Before

I fell asleep I remembered what you told me before you died. You said, "We've had a lot of fun and an intensely loving relationship. We have no unresolved issues and there isn't any guilt for you to carry around. In death, you gave me life. Thank you for taking such good care of me."

I'll say so long for a little while.

I love you.

Susan

Chapter 11

There Was No Safe Place or Comfort Zone As A Hospice Nurse Said She Was Afraid To Bring Her Baby Home And A Wife Who Expressed The Same Concerns About Her Husband

"Life is passion. Passion is energy. Energy is life."

April 1999

Dear Jeff,

You know Jeff that I have been afraid many times in my life. I was frightened when we had to get married because I was pregnant. I wasn't prepared for the responsibilities of what being a wife and mother entailed. I loved you but I wasn't in love with you. We were both afraid of the sacrifices we would have to make. Sometimes I was afraid that our constant arguments would cause you to leave and at other times I was afraid of being alone. But, as the years went by and our friendship grew stronger, it wasn't my marriage that I became more confident with but the security of our long term relationship and what we both could contribute to that "merger." We were a team and we were stronger together than apart. I also became more aware that my fears of loosing you to another man would never happen. I knew that like I knew my own skin. In fact, that one facet of my life became the strongest feeling I had. Oh how I hated your affairs and the other life you were leading, but I continued to love you and allowed our teamwork to make us stronger. We had become partners who depended upon each other. So what if the word co-dependent was a psychological term that maybe cast aspersions and negativity upon a relationship. I knew in my gut that we would never be apart, by choice. It would never be by choice.

Though as stated before, I was afraid of many things along the way. But the word fear took on a completely new meaning and one of gigantic proportions when I first heard about AIDS in 1981. Fear became my soul, heart, spirit, and fear consumed me. Everyday, everything, and everyone you came in contact with made me fearful for you. I was terrified of the possibility that you would come down with this deadly disease. Then in June 1992, when you were diagnosed with pneumonia and AIDS, the fear I experienced at that moment was paralyzing. I was frozen in time. Nothing moved forwards or backwards. I was caught up in the worst nightmare on earth because there was nothing I could do about it. I did not have the power to stop this cruel and vicious disease from taking you from me. I feared for you. I feared for your parents. And I feared over the uncertain and frightening future that would eventually become mine. My fears made me say and do things that I never would have done before. The frustration over the times when I didn't just doubt my ability to help you were real, they were too real. Many times I felt that I was helplessly inadequate to care for myself. Yes, it was fear now that overshadowed any other feeling or emotion that had previously existed.

The following story deals with the issue of fear and tells how 2 extraordinary ladies faced and overcame theirs. They shared with me some personal feelings about their roles as wives, mothers, and caregivers. They helped me to understand why the feelings of uncertainty and doubt can be frightening. Again, as in all these incredible stories, the care center opened up a world of insight to me that never would have happened under any other circumstances. It was a quiet night when I arrived at the center. The atmosphere was peaceful and everything seemed calmer than usual. It was the kind of night that gives hospice a respite from hospice. As I walked past the nurse's station, she greeted me with her beautiful smile. She said, "Hi, Susan. It's nice to see you tonight." Her upbeat cheery voice made everyone around her feel good. She was compassionate, kind, sincere, and always optimistic. She never hesitated when someone would stop and ask her for something. She gave her best to everyone she met, loved her work, and was the perfect hospice nurse. I said, "Hi sweet girl." She responded with, "Just like 3 sugars in coffee." I started going about my rounds, checking on the patients, asking if anyone needed anything.

When I came out of the room I said to the nurse, "I really like the patient in there. It's his wife that I am concerned about. She isn't coping well at the moment." She said, "I'm his nurse. There's something I'd like to talk to you about. Do you have time?" "Of course", I said. She was going to take her break and wanted to sit outside. The evening was warm and balmy with thousands of brilliant stars twinkling down upon us. I said, "There is so much life around us tonight. It is hard to believe that we are at a hospice center." She said, "That man is such a sweet person. He'd been living with prostate cancer for 10 years. He had been at home and was doing well. His pain was under control and his family life was wonderful. About 2 months ago his condition took a turn for the worse and his doctor recommended hospice. Last week, his wife brought him in with an acute episode of pain. It was so unbearable that he couldn't walk, function, or sleep. It took several days to adjust his medications, but he is stable and comfortable again. His doctor said that he would be going home next week and hospice could help over there. His wife said to me, "I am so afraid about him coming home. I've been his caregiver for years, but this is something that I've never experienced before. He is out of pain for now, but what will I do if something like this happens again? What if it's worse than before? He is getting weaker and needs so much help. I feel guilty for feeling this way but I am afraid for him. I don't know if I can handle another crisis. I want him to stay here because I know he will be safe. But, I want him back home with his family. I don't know what to do."

My mind flooded with the images of you coming home from the hospital after your first bout with pneumonia. I remembered how afraid I was for you. It seemed like it happened yesterday instead of 7 years ago. I was caught up in the same conflict and issues that this woman was facing now. My conscious self told me that I would gain confidence in time and would be able to take care of you, but my emotional self was terrified and confused. I questioned everything as I confronted my doubts and fears. The nurse said to me, "I understand why this woman feels this way. She made adjustments as the disease progressed and had times when their life was stable. When her husband's unexpected pain got out of control, she watched him suffer and felt helpless. It's out of fear that she feels inadequate. She is frightened for her husband and for herself. She wants him to stay where he will be safe. Susan, I felt the same way that she does, but for an entirely different reason. I felt this way when I had to take my daughter home from the hospital after she was born." I said, "I don't understand the correlation between your child's birth and the wife's problem. How can you possibly compare the two?" She said, "I've been a nurse for 12 years. I've worked in hospitals and 2 years in a pediatric facility. My husband is also a nurse. We have a wonderful marriage, rewarding careers, and we love kids. We knew from the beginning that we wanted several children. After I suffered two miscarriages, the doctors said that it would be difficult and possibly dangerous for me to get pregnant again. We were devastated.

We had accepted the fact that we might not have any children. However, I did get pregnant and we were both ecstatic and apprehensive at the same time. I had to stay in bed for 9-months, had a Caesarian section, and the baby was perfect. When my husband came to pick us up, I was petrified and started to cry. I panicked. I couldn't stop thinking about the different things that could happen with the baby at home. What if there is an emergency? Will I be able to handle it? This is my baby not someone else's. The hospital gave me a sense of security and well being. It was my safety net. I wanted the baby home, but I was feeling insecure and inadequate. I can relate to this woman's mixed emotions. It was a horrible feeling. My brain told me that this didn't make any sense, but I couldn't convince my emotions to feel the same way. I didn't have a safe place in my heart or a comfort zone in my mind. My uncertainty and doubt lasted for days. Slowly my feelings of inadequacy started to give way to the joyous feelings of motherhood. I became a mother first and a nurse second. I knew that we would be all right." After she told me her story, I understood why both these women felt the way they did. Though their reasons for feeling this way were different, their emotions were the same.

I said, "My husband was ill for a long time. During the different phases of the disease, I was terrified. I didn't know what to expect and I didn't know if I could give him the best care. I was afraid for him and for myself. I didn't have any guidelines or a book telling me about what problems I might run into or how to deal with an emergency or crisis. I had every reason to feel uncertain, vulnerable, and to doubt my capabilities. When he first came home from the hospital I didn't know if I would be able to handle all his medications, the treatments, and the new and complex issues that a long-term illness could present. I knew that while he was in the hospital he would get the care he needed. I wanted him back home, yet I was afraid for his safety and well being. It took me months to gain the confidence I needed to feel comfortable being a primary caregiver. Whenever something unforeseen or unexpected happened I would panic. On several occasions I had to call the doctor or take him to the hospital. The more I learned about taking care of him, the better and more confident I became at giving care. And the more I faced my fears, the stronger I became." She thanked me for listening and I thanked her for sharing her feelings. We smiled, gave each other a hug, and said goodnight until next week.

On the way home, I couldn't stop thinking about our conversation. The nurse addressed the similarities in a way that made me aware of my vulnerability and how important the feelings of security and safety were for me. The fact that she understood this problem from her own perspective made this issue even more powerful. In the beginning, I didn't know anything about the different stages of a long-term illness. In time, I developed the skills and techniques to handle almost anything that could happen. More importantly, what I did learn about myself and the information that I've acquired through my involvement with hospice has helped me to handle my life more effectively. I thought about how many people have experienced this kind of fear. How many would face this issue and doubt their competency? When you watch someone you love face the challenges of a long-term illness, it is normal to feel insecure and fearful. Jeff, your trust in me gave me the confidence I needed to help you through this time. Your unconditional support throughout our marriage and now, even after your death, has helped me to grow stronger and feel more secure. Thank you for trusting me with your life.

I'll say so long for a little while.

I love you.

Susan

Chapter 12

A Wife Who Feels Like She Is Starving Her Husband To Death But He Doesn't Have The Strength, Energy, Or Appetite To Eat

"Once you lived to eat. Now you eat to survive."

May 1999

Dear Jeff,

I'll be 53 years old, tomorrow, May 4th. My birthdays have never been the same since you've died and I don't care very much about them anymore. Tomorrow was supposed to be a special day that celebrated my birth, but for me it's just another day that I won't be spending with you. My birthdays were special because you made them that way. You took me to Hawaii 4 years in a row for my birthday. When I said that I wanted to do something different next year, you bought me a house instead. In fact, over the years, you bought me two homes, 2 cars, and the most beautiful and thoughtful presents I've ever gotten. I will never celebrate a birthday again the way I did with you. Remember the surprise party you gave me for my 30th birthday. It was 1975 and we had built our first home in Houston. You didn't know any of our "cul de sac" neighbors, but you went around to every house on the block introducing yourself. You said that you wanted to invite them to my surprise birthday party. When everyone arrived, I didn't know a soul and you couldn't remember their names or what houses they lived in. Talk about a surprise party. You were incredible and the party was a huge success.

I spent several birthdays alone because you were out of town. But, you always had the card ready before you left, called that day, sent additional cards, and brought me back a gift. We celebrated when you got home. You spoiled me with gifts of perfume, sunglasses, jewelry, and my favorite item, magnets. The only birthday I try not to think about was the one before you died, but as with the other stories in this book, it was last night at the center and a conversation I had with a woman that brought back those painful memories of May 4th, 1994. This book was meant to bring back not only the good times but some of the rougher ones. However, it had to be written no matter how it pulled at my heartstrings. The woman in this story shared with me her feelings of rejection, guilt, and the frustrations she faced as she tried to get her dying husband to eat. The image of my last birthday with you was as vivid now and it was 5 years ago and now it was playing out between two strangers sharing a similar situation. The night of my birthday you wanted to take me to our favorite Italian restaurant. We ordered dinner and when the food came you were too tired and nauseous to eat. When we got home, you said that you would have a piece of birthday cake. I put a candle on your piece and when I asked you to make a wish and blow it out, you couldn't. You didn't have the energy. You took a forkful of cake and threw it up an hour later. You were deathly ill on my last birthday and died three months later. Birthdays have never felt the same. Oh, how this woman got to me with her story and what a frustrating issue many will have to face.

The night was warm and it was still light outside when I got to the center. The late afternoon sun was shining through the white shutters in the hallway. There was a woman leaning against the wall impeccably dressed in a navy blue pinstriped suit. The gold buttons on her jacket twinkled like stars in the sky. As I passed by, she removed a pink handkerchief from under her watch and started to cry. I came over and said, "Hello, my name is Susan. I'm the volunteer on tonight. If you need another handkerchief I always carry an extra one in my pocketbook. They come in very handy around here." She smiled at me and said, "My husband is not eating or drinking anything! How can he get better if he won't eat or drink? I want him to stay alive, but I feel like I am letting him starve to death. What can I do? I feel guilty and helpless." Her sadness was heartbreaking. I said, "I've heard that many times before. It's horrible to watch someone you love refuse to eat or be unable to do so. There is nothing that compares to the feeling of helplessness when your loved one does not want to eat. Your frustrations are overwhelming and there's nothing that you can do about it. It's been a long and painful ordeal for your husband and for you."

I asked her if she would like to get a cup of coffee. "Yes, she said, all I do now is listen to him breath." We got our coffee and sat down. She took out a fresh handkerchief from her purse and wiped her eyes. She said, "It's been a wonderful marriage for 51 years. We've got three great kids and 6 grandchildren. Two years ago my husband was diagnosed with advanced pancreatic cancer. There wasn't much that the doctors could do for him. He tried several drugs and chemotherapy and for a while he was improving. But, his appetite continued to decrease and he was loosing weight. I begged him to eat. I made him everything he ever liked. It didn't matter what time of the day or night. If he said he wanted the littlest thing, I would have gotten it. But, he kept wanting less and less. He just kept pushing the food away saying that he didn't want to eat. What could I do? I didn't want to argue about food any more. About 6 months ago everything took a turn for the worst. He lost a lot of weight, didn't have any energy, and wanted to sleep all the time. Our doctor referred him to hospice."

I said, "May I ask you something personal?" "Yes," she replied. "When your husband told you that he didn't want to eat any longer, what did he say to you?" He said, "All you do is talk about food. Why won't you let me be? I don't want to eat or drink. Don't you know that I would eat if I could? Please stop trying to get me to eat. I would leave the room in tears. Was he giving up? Didn't he want to live? I only wanted to do something for him. I love him. I felt useless and helpless. He chose not to eat before and now he is too weak to take a sip of water. It's harder than I ever imagined." I said, "You gave your husband the greatest gift of all. You're a loving wife and a strong courageous caregiver because you respected your husband's wishes. I felt the same way when my husband was ill. I tried everything to get his appetite to improve. I prayed that he would put on weight. In the beginning, his appetite did improve and he regained his strength. But after two years of fighting the disease, the food portions continued to get smaller and his weight dropped significantly. The time came when he didn't want to eat and there wasn't anything I could do about it. It was part of the illness and the dying process. All I could do was watch and wait. I understand how frustrated and saddened you are. May I tell you what my husband said to me about 2 months before he died?"

He said, "Susan, I'm the patient and the only one who can understand what is happening to me. I don't care about food. My body is rejecting everything. Do you think that a little food or water is going to change anything? Eating will only prolong my suffering. I know that you don't see it that way. You focus now on food because you want me to get better. But, I'm not going to get better. You can't get me to live. The more you talk about food, the more I turn away and tell you no. How can I make you understand that I have no appetite and the thought of eating makes me want to throw up? I feel badly because I know that you are frightened. You want me to eat because you love me. But, this is not the kind of love I need from you now. I've had to give up so much control over my life, but I can still decide if I want to eat or not. Please try to understand that this is one of the few choices I still have left. This is my wish and I want you to respect it." I continued, "He knew that he wanted to die and nothing I said or did could get him to eat. Eventually he was too weak to eat and needed his energy just to breathe. It was agony for me." She said, "I never thought much about the expression, do you live to eat or eat to live until now. I know that I did everything I could. Thank you for your kindness and understanding. Good night." She gave me a hug and walked back towards the room.

The food and nutrition issue is very complex because of the many factors involved. It's the most difficult and stressful issue that a family member will face. During this time, people will say and do anything to get their loved one to eat. Since food is associated with life, when the patient refuses nourishment, it's a painful reminder that their loved one is dying. The family can exhibit feelings of rejection, frustration, sadness, anger, hate, guilt, and fear. The patient and the family are frustrated and everyone is tense, anxious, and emotionally exhausted. Unfortunately, the patient and the family have different reasons for their conflict. Food is also associated with health and well being. The patient's loss of appetite and weight points out how tired their body is from the disease. It's ironic that the patient does not see their loss of appetite and weight as an issue. Their body is shutting down and letting go.

Many times the person does not feel like they have given up, though the family may perceive this as a sign that their loved one has. What the body is saying is that it needs to save its energy for other things. The body doesn't require as much food and water to maintain itself. It is equipped to handle and adjust to the gradual slowing down of its functions. Their body is preparing them for the dying process and they are giving themselves permission to die. As the patient's requirements of food and water decrease, it is important that you let them tell you what they want. It is their choice and you should respect their wishes. This will not be an easy thing to do, but no amount of guilt, manipulation, threats, or crying will change the outcome. You are saddened because you are loosing them, however, the more you try to interfere with the dying process, the harder it becomes. When the end is near, the greatest gift you can give your loved one is to allow them to die comfortably. That's the way they wanted it to be. I hope I respected your wishes.

I'll say so long for a little while.

I love you.

Susan

Chapter 13

How A Breast Cancer Survivor For 15 Years Was Able To Focus On The Present And Enjoy Every Day That She Had Left

"Each day is a gift. That's why it's called a present."

June 1999,

Dear Jeff,

You were a wonderful caregiver. That's one of the reasons why I miss you so much. You never failed to be there for me. Now, when I don't feel well or if I think that there is something wrong, I wish you were here. I depended upon you and I trusted you. I've had some medical problems since you've passed away, but nothing has been critical or long term in nature. Facing my health concerns alone has been a difficult challenge, but it has helped me to gain strength and confidence in myself. My greatest fear remains that if I am ever told that I have a life-threatening illness, I will have to face it alone. If a doctor said to me, "I have some bad news, your test results are back and you have a life-threatening illness." How would I handle this information? What would I do after the numbing shock had worn off and the cruel reality of this nightmarish time had begun? Could I accept this information? Would I deny the doctor's words, desperately trying to convince myself that this couldn't be happening to me?

As my uncertain and frightening future unfolded, would I ever know another moment's peace? How would I begin to take charge of my life and how would I get my emotional self back on track? Would I question the doctor hoping that his diagnosis was incorrect? Would I get a second opinion, a third, or a fourth? What would the treatments involve? What would my alternatives be? Did I catch it in time or was it too late? How long did I have? Would I think that this was the end and that I would I see my life passing before my eyes? Who would I tell and whom could I count on? If the treatments worked and my disease went into remission, would I continue to think that I was going to die? Even if I felt well, would I be able to put the disease and these frightening thoughts out of my mind? How and where would I get the strength to go on? These are some of the difficult and powerful questions I would have to ask myself if I were told that I had a life-threatening illness.

I knew that you were playing Russian roulette with your health. I think that a part of you thought that you would never get AIDS, while another part lived each day knowing that you would. Since most of the men you were promiscuous with had died, how could you possibly escape the HIV virus and not develop AIDS? When our doctor came to the house on June 19th, 1992, and told us that you had PCP, the pneumonia associated with AIDS, his words hit us like a freight train. Our intellectual self told us that we were informed and prepared in case you became ill, but our emotional side was not ready to hear this dreaded diagnosis. You were already critically ill and you didn't have many options available. Drugs were limited and the treatments were even fewer. Much of the data was speculation and unproven because patients didn't live long enough for conclusive studies to be evaluated. Though the outlook for managing HIV and AIDS has improved, there is still no vaccine or cure today. You might have lived longer and had better quality of life if you contracted the disease today, but the road ahead of you would still be long and difficult.

You went through difficult medical procedures, uncomfortable treatments, and took multiple medications with harmful side effects. You tried conventional and unconventional therapies including relaxation techniques, homeopathy, acupuncture, and juicing. You tried to remain positive, hopeful, doing whatever you could to stay optimistic. We continued to travel, to be with family and friends, and maintained as much stability and normalcy in our lives, as possible. But the dark cloud of this horrific disease loomed over our heads every day. The slightest symptom was a terrible reminder of the seriousness of this disease. Your illness was on your mind and in your body every minute of every day for 2 years. Last night at the center, I met a woman who showed great strength and courage as she brought up many of the same issues that you had to deal with when you were ill. She told me how she was able to survive a long-term life threatening illness for 15 years. She spoke about her fears and her expectations and explained how she able to put the disease out of her mind. How did she keep such a positive attitude living with the disease for so long?

When I entered the room, she was propped up against several pillows. She was a large woman and her body took up the entire hospital bed. Her massive appearance was not what I usually saw at the center. There were pictures everywhere. They were on the walls, the tables, taped to the headboard, and on the food tray. I said, "Hello, my name is Susan. I'm a volunteer. May I get you another picture frame?" She laughed. "No, thank you, she said, there's no more room. Would you please inform my nurse that I am ready for my pain medication? I am feeling very agitated." She didn't ask me to get her nurse. She announced it. She was eloquent, articulate, and had a sophisticated air about her. I said, "I'll go and get your nurse." I told her nurse that she needed her assistance and went back into the room. I asked her if she would like some company. She said, "If they ever bring me my anxiety pill, I'll be happy to chat. I get so damn anxious. My brain is telling me that I am doing fine, but it can't seem to convince my nerves. A part of me is accepting, while the other part is in denial. It's the denial part that wants the drugs."

She laughed at herself and her sense of humor made me feel comfortable. I pulled up a chair and said, "You speak beautifully. You're an English teacher aren't you?" Yes, she said. I've loved teaching for 30 years. My family and students have been encouraging and totally supportive. But, I'm tired now and it's time to take my retirement. I've lived with this damn disease for 15 years and I never quit fighting. Everything happened so unexpectedly. I was taking a shower when I found the lump in my right breast. I was 40 years old. I knew it was cancer. I turned off the water and stood there. My heart stopped. I felt absolute fear and panic for the first time in my life. I sat down on the shower floor and cried. I totally lost control. I can't remember how long I sat there. Finally I got out of the shower and looked at my breasts. Of course, there was nothing to see. My first reaction was that it was my imagination. They looked normal. But, I felt my breast again and the lump was there. I called my doctor and made an appointment.

My doctor felt the lump and scheduled me for an ultrasound and biopsy. The results came back as I'd expected. The mass was small and malignant. My doctor suggested that I have a mastectomy. Within one month my world had collapsed. I changed from a happy, fun-loving, career oriented human being to a paranoid, shocked, disbelieving, basket case. The doctor removed my right breast and was confident that radiation and chemotherapy treatments would be successful. They said my prognosis for a full recovery was good. I went through the treatments with some discomfort but it wasn't as difficult as I had anticipated. I lost most of my hair but I bought some great wigs. My students liked the fact that I looked "different" a few times a week. Everyone was so wonderful. Four months later, I was healthy, cancer-free, and felt great. Other than the physical reminder of my ordeal, I knew that I was fine. I wasn't going to waste one precious moment dwelling on something that might never happen again. I did what the doctors told me to do, but I wouldn't let this disease control my life. I went back to teaching, traveling, and playing poker. Yes, I love poker and I can play with one breast.

Five years later I was experiencing back pain and had a difficult time walking. The tests revealed that my cancer had reoccurred in my spine. Surgery was not an option. I chose to have chemotherapy and radiation treatments again. After six months, my cancer went into remission. Maybe it was the poker player in me, but I knew the game wasn't over with yet. This might sound simplistic, but I was more afraid to be afraid than to be strong and deal with it. I've never been a "victim" and I despise the word. I went another 10 years without a problem. I focussed on life and lived it. It was a great time for me. I took summers off and traveled. One morning I woke up and couldn't move my legs. The pain was excruciating. The cancer had spread into my bones and spine. I'd done a great job of putting this off for 15 years, but I knew now my time had come."

I said to her, "How did you manage to put it out of your mind all these years?" "It wasn't easy, she said. I did everything imaginable from the conventional treatments to the alternative ones. I tried hypnotism, acupuncture, relaxation techniques, vitamins, exercise, and crystals. I thought that the negative energy from worrying would be more harmful than the disease. I put my faith in the doctors, the medications, my family, and friends. I continued to do the things that made me feel good and I stayed around positive people. Life is a lot like playing poker. You have to know when to play your hand, when to bluff, and when to fold. Now, it's time to fold." I said, "You are incredible. I can't imagine facing anything like this with as much courage and strength as you've shown. I would have loved you for a teacher. Good night."

She was exceptional in the way that she handled her life and managed the disease. She wanted to continue to enjoy the things she'd always known and call the shots for as long as she could. She didn't have any regrets, made her own choices, and never felt sorry for herself. She reminded me so much of you. You both trusted in the same things and did everything that you possibly could to survive. You cherished every day, never gave up on life, and didn't have any regrets. You never let your illness control your life. The disease lived with you every day, but you lived with the disease also. When the time comes that I have to face my own mortality, I hope that I will have the same strength and extraordinary courage that both of you have shown.

I'll say so long for a little while.

I love you.

Susan

Chapter 14

A Daughter Questions Her Fears As She Faces The Issue Is She More Afraid To Leave Her Loved One Or To Come Back

"Fear gripped me every time I said hello or good bye."

July 1999

Dear Jeff,

Why did you have to get sick and die during the summer? It was always our favorite season. We had our most wonderful times taking long leisurely walks on the beach, riding around in our convertible, eating late dinners on warm balmy nights, and lying for hours in the sun as we tried to outdo each other getting magnificent tans. We enjoyed bicycle riding, swimming, and holding each other while dancing under starlit skies. When you were diagnosed with AIDS in June 1992 and after you died in August 1994, all that I had left was a sickening empty feeling in the pit of my stomach. I never thought that I would ever enjoy a summer again without you to share it with. It took me a year to build up enough courage to go to the beach. When I finally did, I had to have a friend go with me. I cried hysterically as I walked that 2-mile stretch at Deerfield Beach because I was not walking it with you. I also never thought that I would ever feel comfortable again in our home. For months I slept on a couch in the den because I couldn't bear to be alone in our bed. As I walked through rooms displaying the beautiful treasures and souvenirs of our life together, I was haunted by the images of your death. In a home that once knew intimacy and love, laughter and joy, I felt cold and alone, unfamiliar and strange.

For 2 years, the disease made me afraid of everything. I was unprepared for what might happen while I was away from you and I never knew what to expect when I came back. Whether you were in the hospital or at home, the fear of what might be when I'd say either hello or good bye to you gripped me to the core. My thoughts were so frightening that I would freeze before I walked into the room. My heart would race and I would break out into a cold sweat, anxious and fearful of what I might have to face. It took every bit of strength for me to smile and say, "Hi baby, I'm back." I might have left you for 30 minutes, but it was enough time for a crisis to develop. What if your condition got worse? What if you spiked another high fever or started to convulse? What if you had thrown up, soiled yourself, or fallen? Would you be too weak to be able to get up? And my greatest fear remained the thought of you dying and that I would not be there for you. I was afraid for myself and I was afraid for you. Last night at the center, I met a woman who was dealing with the same issue. She was afraid to leave her loved one and even more afraid to return. She made me think about the many times when I'd faced this kind of terror and apprehension. As we spoke, her words brought back the memories when I said so long for a little while and didn't know what would await me when I returned.

As I walked down the hallway, the music coming from the room was magnificent. I heard a solo piano concerto so brilliantly and passionately played that I thought someone was performing it in person. As I stood outside the door listening to the piano's beautiful sounds, she was standing near the bed. I watched her slowly lean over and kiss the woman on the lips. I entered the room and heard her say, "I love you Mom. I love you Mom." I approached the girl and said, "Hello. My name is Susan. I'm a volunteer. The beautiful music charmed me into the room. Would you like to be alone with your mother or would you mind me sitting here?" "No, she said, Mom always likes having people around. My sister is a concert pianist. She is the one playing on the tape. She loved to play for my mother. Since she can't be here with us now, she thought that Mom would like this. I've been told that the sense of hearing is the last one that a person looses. Hopefully my mother can still hear my words and my sister's music." I said, "You adore your mother, don't you?" She held her mother's hands and said, "Yes, I do adore her. She is everything and she is my best friend.

My father died 15 years ago and Mom moved to Florida. I lived in New York and after my divorce I wanted to live closer to Mom. We were only 10 minutes from each other. It was like growing up all over again. Several times a week we ate dinner together, went to the movies, shopped, and traveled. When Mom developed liver cancer 3 years ago, I moved into her home. This is the final chapter in our beautiful book of love." The naturalness of a daughter's unconditional love overflowed as she gently and tenderly continued to caress the frail woman's arms and stroke her forehead. The daughter had now assumed the role of the mother and she was the one soothing and comforting the child. She glanced at her watch and said, "I have to be going now. I am so tired and I need to get up early to go to work. I've taken a lot of time off recently. Saying good-bye is the hardest thing for me to do. I am afraid and feel panicked when I have to leave, but I can not stay with her all the time." She continued to kiss her mother telling her how much she loved her. She fought back her tears knowing that she would have to say goodbye. My heart ached for her because I remembered how many times I had said the same good-byes to you when you were ill. I asked her if I could walk her to the car. "Yes, she said, that would be nice."

When we got to her car I said, "May I ask you something personal? It's a question that I've never asked anyone before. However, I think that you might be feeling the same way I felt when my husband was ill." "Of course," she said. I explained, "My husband passed away 5 years ago after a long illness. For 2 years he was in and out of the hospital several times. Hospice came into our home and assisted me with his care during the last 2 months. My question is, do you think that it is more difficult for you to leave your mother at the center now or is it harder for you to come back and see her?" Her immediate response told me that she understood exactly what I meant. She said, "I am miserable and broken-hearted when I have to leave. It is torture not be to with her every moment of the day and night. I feel that I should be with her all the time. The guilt and anguish I go through when I have to leave is horrible. I am afraid that she will die while I am gone. Even during the early stages of her illness, I hated to leave her. Our time together was so special. But, I am also afraid to return because I don't know what I will see when I walk into the room. There were times when I would leave for just a few hours and something would happen. She might be upset or her condition would change. My heart would pound and I'd hold my breath when I saw her again. I hated to leave and I was afraid to come back. I never knew I could feel like this. Both feelings have torn me apart."

I said, "I felt the same way throughout my husband's illness, especially during the last few months. There were times when I needed to leave him for a few hours, but when I'd walk through the door, I was afraid to go into the room. I could leave him feeling comfortable and everything was stable. Then I'd return and a crisis had developed, or something unforeseen and unexpected had happened. I never knew what to expect and it was frightening. Even when people were taking care of him, I hated to leave and I dreaded coming back. How would he look? How would he feel? What if he needed me and I wasn't there? Would he be afraid and feel alone? And what if I wasn't there when he died? It was difficult for me to trust other people with his care. That was a very difficult thing for me to learn to do. I was his wife, his best friend, and his caregiver. I wanted to be with him all the time." She said, "It helps knowing that someone else feels the same way that I do. Loving someone who is gravely ill is unbearably sad for everyone. I understand that it is important to share this time with people who can help, but that doesn't make it any easier emotionally." I said, "You helped me a lot by sharing your feelings. You are a wonderful daughter. Please tell your sister that her beautiful music made everyone feel better. Goodnight."

On the way home all I could think about was what this woman had said to me. Meeting her helped me to understand why I felt the emotional conflict that had troubled me for so long. I knew that my feelings of guilt, fear, anticipation, and sorrow were not only natural but also expected during such a difficult time. This woman and I felt these emotions because we loved deeply and passionately about someone and we didn't want to have to say a final goodbye. We were torn apart and frightened because we loved and we felt helpless in stopping something that we didn't want to ever happen. Both situations caused great emotional conflict and sorrow and neither one was easier than the other one to deal with. I think that the word "secure" and "insecure" best sums up the feelings that are experienced when someone you love is gravely ill, especially when the end is near.

I say that because nothing ever seems stable, long term, or certain during this time. How can you feel safe and secure when you don't know what to expect? It's a frightening feeling that never leaves. Whatever the feelings, they were for the right reasons. We dealt with our fears because we needed to be there for our loved ones and we needed to do it for ourselves. We would have continued to live through our fears as long as we had to. I know that I am grateful for the gift of time. It has helped me to adjust to the reality of coming home alone, going to the beach by myself, and having dinner without you. It helped to heal my wounds and comfort my heart. Though I said good bye to you with my words, I'll never say a final good bye with my heart.

I'll say so long for a little while.

I love you.

Susan

Chapter 15

Pain Comes In Many Ways But For This Woman The Physical Pain Of Her Illness Was So Horrible That She Wanted To Commit Suicide

"Physical pain transcends every other form of pain because it's all-powerful. It can hinder you from growing, paralyze you in the present, and deny you a future. It can hold you back from living or wanting to live."

August 1999

Dear Jeff,

As I write to you, I am in a great deal of pain. It's not like the physical kind that the woman in this story had to endure. My pain is mental and emotional. My mind is tired and my heart is sad. I am in pain because I miss you, my best friend. I need your comfort, your words of encouragement, and your never-ending faith in me. When you died on August 17th, 1994, I never thought that I would be able to function again. I was alive after your death, but I felt like the walking dead. I was numb, a shell housing emptiness, loneliness, and despair. I was exhausted, drained, depleted, and destroyed. The only thing I felt was pain. It has taken me years to learn how to deal with the different kinds of pain and the levels to which they had taken their toll. Yes, I can tell you that I've made some progress in handling my grief and loss. I've healed or at least tried to, gone forward, and most of the time, I am somewhat content with my life. Yet, here it is today, five years after your death that my pain and sorrow continues to trouble me. I cried uncontrollably today because the sadness I feel is horrible. I know that eventually this pain will also pass, but it hurts to hurt and I am hurting now.

I looked up the meaning of the word pain. I hoped that seeing the words and reading their meaning might help to ease the sorrow I was experiencing now. The dictionary explained about the different kinds of pain and to what degree and at what level they were capable of taking control over one's life. The simplest definition of the word pain means physical or mental suffering or distress, especially an unpleasant sensation arising from injury or disease. As I continued reading, it said that pain could be physical, mental, emotional, and spiritual. It was possible to experience them one at a time or all together. The reason that physical pain is the first one that people think of is because physical pain is easily understood. It usually happens at a younger age and leaves a powerful and lasting impression. However, what is the definition of mental pain? Wouldn't it be distress and suffering of the mind? And wouldn't it be just as painful and agonizing to deal with as physical pain? Just because you can not see or touch the terror of mental pain, does it not mean that is any less torturous to endure? Perhaps mental pain is too sensitive or private an issue and many are afraid to speak openly about it for fear that they will be judged or criticized. And why should this be? When the feelings of anguish and torment are locked up inside the mind, does this make the pain any less harmful or destructive? Mental pain cripples and destroys the body and the soul. It is also a pain that one will do anything to be free of.

What is emotional pain? Does this mean that your emotions are suffering or in distress? What could be more emotionally painful than to watch someone you love die a slow horribly vicious death? What words could possibly describe the frustration and agony you are experiencing, as you stand by helplessly unable to stop the inevitable? Aren't you in emotional pain when you grieve your loss while trying desperately to cope with the aftermath? How do you express yourself when you are dealing with emotional pain? Are you able to "remove that intimate and personal part of yourself from you?" Isn't emotional pain something that can keep you in the past, while you are stuck in the present? And isn't emotional pain when you are unable to go forward because you are unsure and frighteningly insecure of the future? Isn't emotional pain when you can't feel the feelings, cope with the issues, or confront the "real you in you?" And aren't you in the greatest emotional pain when you continually restrict yourself within your own insecurities because you are afraid to risk for fear of loosing?

Finally, there is spiritual pain. This pain is the most difficult one to describe because it is intensely personal and deeply private. Perhaps somewhere along the way you lose your faith in a belief system or maybe you never had one to begin with. If you feel empty and alone, when you are void of any peace and contentment, and when there is no harmony in your life, aren't you in spiritual pain? When you want to believe in someone, something, or anything but can not, isn't this spiritual pain? When you brutally question, demanding to know why you aren't strong enough to believe in yourself, isn't that spiritual pain? And when you do not have the strength to carry on and when you want to give up on life itself, isn't that spiritual pain? Spiritual pain is the most difficult one to explore and try to understand because it will make you look into yourself for the answers.

The following story deals with physical pain and how the intensity of this woman's suffering nearly caused her to commit suicide. She would rather have died than to continue living with the endless agonizing pain she had been enduring for months. This was a night and a story I shall never forget nor want to because many more people I will meet in life shall experience the same thing. When I entered her room to collect her dinner tray, I woke her up. She was sleeping in the large recliner with her legs curled up underneath her. I said, "I apologize for disturbing you. My name is Susan and I'm a volunteer." She said, "I can't keep my eyes open. I doze all the time." I said, "Would you like to get into bed?" "No, she responded, but if you'll stay with me, I'll tell you the 99 different ways to sleep in a lounge chair. I'll have plenty of time to sleep later on." I removed the half-eaten dinner tray and came back. She said, "I can't believe that I've been here for a week. Time flies when you are comfortable and out of pain. I don't like feeling sleepy but my nurse said I would adjust to the medication in time."

I said, "Did you come into the center to get your pain under control?" "Yes, she responded. My doctor was wonderful and did the best he could. He never deceived me about my disease. We both knew that I was going to die. But, for several months my pain was so excruciating that I wanted to commit suicide. He couldn't get the pain to stop. I was frozen and paralyzed from it. I felt like I was already dead, yet I was experiencing the agony of the disease and my life. I told my doctor that I couldn't take it anymore. He said that my only other choice was hospice. Since I've been here, I feel like a different person. The pain is finally gone. I used to hear about quality of life, but when you don't have any, life doesn't exist any longer. I wish I had come here sooner."

I said, "What were you diagnosed with?" She responded, "I was diagnosed with cervical cancer. I'd been going every year for a pap-smear and never had a bad report. Two years ago, the results came back positive. When I went in for another pap, it came back suspicious. My doctor said that there wasn't any cause for alarm and told me to come back in 3 months. Now the results indicated cervical cancer. I was only 43 years old. How could this have happened? One day I was healthy, active, vital, and alive. I had a successful real estate career and everything in the world to live for.

I had a hysterectomy followed by chemotherapy and radiation. I was nauseous and lost my hair. But, I was able to tolerate the physical pain. I started getting my confidence back and felt that I would be beat the odds. Well, I didn't. Six months ago the disease spread into my liver and pancreas. I was physically, mentally, emotionally, and spiritually destroyed. I questioned God, my emotional stability, my relationships, and my life. But, it wasn't until the physical pain became so intolerable that I said no more. The physical pain took over my life. It controlled everything. My body ached so badly that I couldn't think or breathe. My heart would pound with every surge of pain. When I was in the hospital, the drugs couldn't stop it. There was nothing I could do. I came home and said I would kill myself rather than put up with this. I told my doctor and he referred me to hospice. I am thankful that I can fall asleep because I am not in any pain. It isn't how long you have to live, but how well you live. I don't want to take my life anymore. God can have it when he is ready."

I said, "I'm glad that you are out of pain and have some quality back in your life." She said, "Please wake me up any time. I'm ready to get into bed. Thank you." We gave each other a hug and I wished her a good night's sleep. For those suffering through the constant agony of physical pain, they will do anything to be free from it. Some may wish to die while others will take their own life. This woman's story points out that life as well as death should be treated with respect. The person dealing with the pain should be understood and treated with compassion. If quality of life is most important, then whether you see pain, feel pain, or think pain, pain hurts and it hurts to hurt. I don't know Jeff how you managed to endure the continuous torture of your body, mind, and spirit for so long. You stayed strong and courageous as you fought every day for two years to live. Until your last breath, you never hated or blamed anyone. You never said that you wanted to die and you never asked me to end your life. You knew that if you had asked me to, I would have. There will never be a reason why someone's final days shouldn't be free of pain and have some quality.

When the agony is so overwhelming that someone wants to die, how do you encourage him or her to want to live? When the pain is so intense that life means nothing, what words could possibly make any difference? Perhaps the words, "I know another way that might be better for you. You should know about hospice. Hospice is a choice and a chance and you are the only one who should decide what is best for you. Hospice changes everything but interferes with nothing. It changes the living process and the way a person feels about their life." I know Jeff that you spent your final days the way you chose. My emotional pain will continue to lessen in time, but it will never go away. I miss you.

I will say so long for a little while.

I love you.

Susan

Chapter 16

A Woman With Terminal Lung Cancer Had To Slowly Give Up Everything She Loved But She Managed To Have Fun And Keep Some Control By Having Her Daily Cigarette And Would Smoke Until She Could Never Hold A Cigarette Again

"I've never met anyone but you who could make fun feel so easy and right."

September 1999,

Dear Jeff,

At one of your workshops, a student asked what you thought the meaning of the word fun meant. You said, "The meaning of the word fun is relative. It means different things at different times for different reasons to different people. Fun can last a few moments, an hour, a day, a week, a month, a year, or a lifetime. Fun doesn't have to involve doing something. It can be fun doing nothing at all. You don't have to be with someone to have fun. You can have it all by yourself. Having fun is an attitude and a choice." You lived your life by the words you spoke and it was that energy and zest for life that kept our marriage together for a wonderfully fun 25 year adventure. You made me laugh and you energized me. I remembered another seminar when you gave the participants a need's assessment test. The test was to determine which of the following needs were your strongest and which were not as important. The needs were fun, freedom, worth and recognition, and power. There weren't any wrong or right answers and it wasn't a pass or fail test. You thought that it would be interesting for us to take it along with the class. There were 100 questions on various subjects and situations. When the tests were evaluated, we agreed on 99 out of the 100 questions. Our strongest need was for fun, the second was freedom, the third was worth and recognition, and the fourth was power. The test validated something that we already knew. When it came to having fun, we made the perfect couple.

A few weeks ago, I met a special lady at the care center that reminded me of you. She said the same thing to me about having fun that you used to say. She said, "If you have to ask yourself if you are having fun, then you probably aren't having any." She had slowly given up everything that she liked to do, but she still managed to have fun doing the one thing that she liked doing the best. She spoke to me openly and candidly about what having fun meant to her at this time in her life. She was a woman who wanted to maintain her independence, to make her own decisions, and to have fun for as long as she could. When I went into the room to answer her call button, she wasn't what I expected to see. She was sitting in the lounge chair wearing a hot pink turban and black Harley-Davidson sunglasses. She couldn't have weighed more than 90 pounds and was hooked up to a portable IV monitor. Her oxygen line was all tangled up and lying next to her on the floor. She was having difficulty breathing and I assumed that she was calling for help. What made this experience so special was the fact that I was wearing a hot pink turban just like hers. I'd seen other patients wearing turbans, but she completely caught me off guard. When we realized that we were both wearing the same color turbans, we burst out laughing.

She started gasping for air and laughing at the same time. I put the oxygen line back in her nose, turned off the call button and waited for her to settle down. I said, "My name is Susan and I'm a volunteer. I love your turban. Having a bad hair day like me or do you just like looking exotic?" She said in a deep throaty voice, "Take me out for a cigarette." She didn't ask me. She commanded me. I said, "You look more like you should be smoking a cigar rather than a cigarette. Would you like to go for a ride on your motorcycle too? Don't go away. I'll check with your nurse and be right back." She was eccentric, outrageous, and determined. I said to her nurse, "The interesting woman with the turban and sunglasses wants to have a cigarette. Is she allowed to smoke?" "Oh, yes, the nurse said. She has emphysema and lung cancer, but she's not going to give up her cigarettes. She can take the IV outside on the patio and she doesn't need the oxygen all the time. You'll have to light her cigarettes and stay with her."

I went back and said to the woman, "Okay, let's light up. You're out of here." I hung the oxygen tube over the chair, dragged the portable monitor with us, and went outside. The ashtray was full of Marlboro cigarette butts and a large bowl of water served as a makeshift fire extinguisher. Though it continued to get dark, she did not take her sunglasses off. I watched as she slowly removed a gold cigarette lighter and holder from a matching case. She could barely get the cigarette to her lips, but when I lit that cigarette and she took her first drag, her expression said it all. I could see the pleasure that she derived from smoking. I said, "You look very glamorous with your cigarette holder and your sunglasses on." "Yes, she responded, I think elegance and style are something that you are born with. By the way, I sold the motorcycle a year ago." "So, I said, what brings you here?"

She said, "I'm 64 years old. I've been smoking since I've been 11. Ten years ago, I was diagnosed with emphysema. The doctor said that I should stop smoking. I tried that for 1 hour and said that the torture wasn't worth it. I continued to smoke. I needed oxygen once in a while and couldn't do some of the physical things I used to do, but I felt good. Gradually it became more difficult to breathe and I started getting dizzy. About 2 years ago, I passed out in the yard. I was taken to the hospital and they discovered a malignant mass in my lung. They operated, followed up with chemotherapy and radiation, but nothing helped. They said that I had a year to live. The cancer has finally spread throughout my body. Slowly I had to give up my job, my activities, my fun, my freedom, and all the other things that made my life worth living. Finally, there was only one thing left for me to enjoy and I wasn't going to give that pleasure up. I would continue to smoke until I couldn't hold a damn cigarette any longer. My family, friends, and the doctors could stand on their heads and spit nickels, but I wouldn't give it up. It's the one thing that I have to look forward to. It doesn't take much anymore to make me happy but I'm still going to try. I chose to have fun all my life and dying isn't going to change a thing."

I said, "If you want to smoke when I am at the center, please ring. I'd be happy to sit with you. It's been difficult having to give up everything that made your life yours. I understand why you feel the way that you do and I respect you for it. There are many people just like you who feel the same way." She said, "My family doesn't understand how a woman with lung cancer and emphysema could still choose to smoke." I said, "Smoking is your pleasure and it brings you happiness. It's also allowing you to maintain your independence, to make your own decisions, and to keep control of your life." We spent a lot of time together over the next few weeks. I came by everyday for an hour, lit her cigarettes and watched her smoke. Every time she lit up she was reinforcing her passion for life and her ability to take control of it. We laughed and we cried as she told me about her life, her interests, her family, and her fears. She accepted the fact that she was dying and she was at peace with herself. She knew how to enjoy life, people, and didn't have any regrets. She was independent, had a wonderful sense of humor, and she was fun.

That's why she reminded me so much of you. She opened up a subject that I had been dealing with for a long time and she helped me to understand how important it was for you to do the things that you wanted to do. Your life was filled with fun, passion, and enthusiasm for 47 years. I know now why you didn't want to get tested for HIV. You couldn't have lived each day to the fullest if you knew that you were positive and that you might become symptomatic with AIDS at any time. It would have disrupted and interfered with your need for fun and it would have diminished the quality of your fun time. It would have destroyed the way you lived your life and what you lived for. That was the saddest and cruelest part of the disease. As it slowly progressed, you were forced to give up so many things that you loved to do. Traveling became difficult, eating was a chore, exercising was impossible, and you watched yourself become someone you didn't know or want to be. It stripped you of life's pleasures while it robbed you of your greatest need of all. I watched as your need for freedom and independence gradually disappeared and I stood by helplessly as your need for worth and recognition gave way to tolerance and acceptance.

Your life had become one of compromise and dependency. But, there was one need that you held on to until the end. It was your need for power. You were not going to relinquish your control over that. There was a time when your need for power was secondary. Now it was the only one that mattered. You were just like this woman. You chose to do something that you wanted to do until you died. You would call the shots, control your fate, and would not allow the disease to destroy whatever pride and dignity you had left. You chose to die at home with hospice there to help us. You had the power to decide till the very end what was best for you. I remembered when we were walking on a beach in Hawaii several years ago and I asked you if you wanted to be a millionaire. You said, "If it means not having fun, then I'd rather be poor." I said, "But, what about people who are workaholics? Don't you think that they are having fun even though they might be working all the time? Just because you think that eating out, shopping, going to the movies, traveling, and lying in the sun are fun things to do, does that mean that people who constantly work aren't having fun?" You said, "My life is fun because I choose to make it that way. Having fun is a personal thing. It should be easy and I shouldn't have to think about it. If you like what you do then financial rewards always happen." "Okay, I said, we are rich in fun and semi-rich financially. I can settle for that."

I'll say so long for a little while.

I love you.

Susan

Chapter 17

How A Hospice Nurse Was Able To Separate Her Personal Life From Her Professional One As She Dealt With Her Husband's Illness And Death And Came Back To Hospice To Help Others

"I had to detach myself from us before I could remove myself from me and move on."

October 1999

Dear Jeff,

On August 17th, 1994, the wonderful life that I thought would last forever had finally and tragically come to an end. After your death, I was raw, vulnerable, and drowning in pain. My days became lonely empty endless hours of heartache and despair. The smallest thing could send me running, crying hysterically to the safety and solitude of a cold and lonely bedroom. I wanted to shut myself off from the world, but my attempt to escape my sorrow and agony proved useless and futile. I could not run away and hide from myself. I never realized how traumatic the long-term effects of your illness had been on me. Everything I saw reminded me of the horrible disease you had to endure. I stopped watching programs on television that dealt with illness, tragedy, or loss. I avoided listening to any kind of music for fear that a song would remind me of the past and bring back a beautiful memory of the life that I once shared with you. I couldn't go the movies because there might be a scene that would cause me to loose control even though I sat in a darkened theater surrounded by the company of strangers. I placed our photo albums in a storage box and gathered up the dozens of videos we took during our many fun-filled exciting vacations. These remembrances were too painful to endure.

I tried getting involved with organizations that helped people living with AIDS. I hoped that the information I'd acquired through my experiences over those past 2 years might assist others who were going through similar situations. But, the horror as I watched these people face their ordeal and the visible signs of the disease was intolerable and impossible for me to do. I had to avoid being around anyone who looked ill. Loosing you was even more painful because I was a caregiver and nurturer by nature. I loved being a homemaker, your wife, and I enjoyed knowing that I was good at helping you. I liked being part of a team. I thrived on the responsibility of taking care of our home and being there for you. Your thanks and appreciation for doing the things that I chose to do felt wonderful. I needed you to need me and you did. However, taking care of a loved one who is seriously ill is not the same thing as taking care of others on a daily basis. If my frustrations were that overwhelming both during your illness and after your death, how painfully difficult it must be for someone who is trained to do this professionally. This story is about an incredibly strong and courageous nurse who had to deal with this issue. She was taught to help, to heel, and to assist people in their time of need, yet when a life threatening illness happened to her husband, she felt helpless and hopeless. She spoke to me about the problems she'd experienced when she went back to work and how difficult it was to assist people again after her loss.

This story did not happen at the hospice care center but while I was on my way to visit my parents in Albany, New York. It was their understanding at this time and their unconditional love and support that I really needed now. While waiting for my flight, I noticed a woman wearing the same red hospice heart pin on her collar as I was. I found myself staring at her because she was strikingly beautiful. Her dark brown hair was cut very short and her flawless olive complexion made her look healthy and athletic. When she realized that I was staring at her, she smiled at me. Her smile was warm and sincere. I walked over to her and said, "I couldn't help but notice that you are wearing a Hospice Heart pin. We have great taste in designer jewelry. My name is Susan. I'm a volunteer at a hospice care center in Boca Raton." She extended her hand and said, "I'm a hospice nurse in Ft. Lauderdale. Do you have this pin in all the latest colors?" "Oh yes, I responded. They were having a sale on them and I bought a rainbow of shades." We laughed because we both knew that the pins were free.

I said, "What time is your flight?" She responded, "I've got an hour before I board." "Me too, I said. Let's get a cup of coffee." She asked me why I got involved with hospice. I said, "My husband died from AIDS. He was ill for two years and hospice helped at home during the final weeks. I didn't know anything about hospice until this happened. Now, besides being at the center,

I write stories about issues that others are going through as they face similar situations." She said, "You went through a lot didn't you?" "Yes, I said. It was the most difficult thing I could ever have imagined. I didn't know if I would survive after his death. Now, I know that hospice will always be in my life." She said, "I was a hospice nurse at a care center in Ft. Lauderdale for 8 years when my husband was diagnosed with pancreatic cancer. We had just celebrated 20 wonderful years of marriage and renewed our wedding vows on a 10-day Alaskan cruise. When he was first diagnosed, I was thankful that I knew so much about this disease and was able to help him. I understood the dimension of his condition and felt fortunate that he could depend on me during his treatments. I was able to help him both as his wife and a nurse. I adjusted my schedule to accommodate his needs and for three years we managed to get through some difficult times.

As my husband's condition deteriorated, it became more physically, mentally, and emotionally exhausting for me to be at work and to perform my nursing duties. I felt like a robot, functioning only on command. Every day I saw the horrible future in front of me. When I knew that his death was eminent and he finally needed hospice help, I found it impossible to deal with. I felt frustrated, helpless, and worst of all, hopeless. I wanted to do something more for him, but I couldn't. I helped others but I couldn't help him and I wasn't able to help myself. After he died, I threw myself into my work. I didn't want to be at home thinking. I didn't want the intense feeling of frustration causing me to remember the ordeal I'd just been through. I thought that the only way for me to deal with my loss was to give everything to my career and to the people I could still help. Six months later, I had a breakdown. I collapsed at work and had to take a leave of absence. I was exhausted, burnt out, and on a path of self-destruction. I hadn't taken the time to separate the professional nurse from the personal wife. I had to deal with what had happened, decide what I wanted to do with the rest of my life, and take care of myself.

It took a year for me to decide that I truly loved nursing and helping people. I also loved hospice because I understood the needs of people at this time. I couldn't change the outcome, but as a wife, nurse, and caregiver, I made his journey a little more bearable. I lost my husband and best friend, but my understanding of this experience has made me stronger and I am a better nurse now because of it." I said, "I've heard this from other professionals. Feelings and emotions take precedent over everything else and rationalizing is useless when the heart is involved. Your training is valuable and your experience is something that others will benefit from. I'm glad that you found out what you wanted and that you chose to go back to your profession. I waited two years before I decided to go into hospice work. It's still difficult to be in certain situations, but I know that I can help others as I continue to heal myself. We wear our red heart hospice pins proudly." With that, we heard our flights being announced, hugged, and said good-bye. Hospice professionals are special and unique. They are sensitive, compassionate, and understanding. They give to others honestly in a way that only true "caregiving" people can do. Though they've been trained to handle end of life situations, how do they deal with their own frustrations when they watch their loved one pass away? How do they detach or remove themselves from the professional self when this experience becomes painfully personal? When the person who is dying just isn't a patient any longer, how do they cope with the grief after their loss? How will they keep it together when their emotions rage out of control? How will they handle the feelings of helplessness and hopelessness? They will handle it in their own way and in their own time, just as everyone has to do. Everyone has their own way of coping with death and grief. Until it happens to you, you will not know how much you will be able to handle. You will be challenged and you will survive, even when you feel that you will not. People will want to help and comfort you, but you have to choose very carefully whom you let close to you and what you expose yourself to during this time.

    I did not know how long my grieving process would take or what to expect. I couldn't anticipate what might happen next because I didn't know what my future would involve now that you were gone. My only consolation was in the fact that your pain and suffering was finally over. I felt a sense of completion because I had been there for you during your life and assisted you until the end. Training people to save, heal, and cure cannot stop the heart from feeling. You once said to me, "Susan, I will never get AIDS because you take such good care of me." We believed that once in a while, didn't we? How could you give me so much credit? I was able to help you for 25 years as a wife, friend, caregiver, and caretaker, but I could not stop you from dying. I could give you quality of life, help you to maintain your dignity and pride, and did many things for you that needed to be done. But, nothing could stop the disease from taking your life. You trusted me with your care and I know that I did the best that I could to make your life and especially your last days, as good as they could be. Thank you for allowing me to give care, to take care, and for trusting me. Time has helped me in every way, especially since I invested the time in myself and gave my Hospice Heart to others.

I'll say so long for a little while.

I love you.

Susan

Chapter 18

A Woman Converted To Catholicism At The Care Center And Said That Until Her Last Breath It Was Never To Late To Make Something Good Happen

"You never put off living, but you put off knowing about your life."

November 1999

Dear Jeff,

We were having dinner one evening when the subject of paying the bills and balancing the checkbook came up. You know how you hated doing this and your procrastination always got me upset. I started yelling trite little expressions at you like, "Never put off tomorrow what you can do today. A bird in the hand is worth two in the bush. A penny saved is a penny earned. Life is a gift and today is a present." You politely excused yourself from the table and walked away. I stormed around the kitchen and later apologized. I hadn't thought about that evening until yesterday when I met a family at the care center who addressed the issue of time and the importance of it. They helped me to appreciate you even more because you always had your priorities straight. You knew what was most important in life. You never failed to do the things that really mattered. Though they seemed so at the time, as I look back now, it was not important that you put off doing chores like taking out the trash, putting your clothes away, bathing the dog, doing yard work, and yes reading anything other than menus and travel brochures. You always got everything done on time, but you did them when you were ready to.

I am sorry that I put so much pressure on you to live your life according to my schedule and my time frame. When it came to the important "issue things," you handled them immediately and you never complained or avoided the responsibility they involved. You never put off loving your parents and cherished any opportunity to get together with them. You never put off giving your clients and your career the very best you could. You never put off your friends when they needed you. You never put off remembering special occasions or celebrating joyous events. You never put off anything that gave quality to our life. You never put off having fun. You never put off dining out, going to the movies, the theater, the ballet, and traveling. And, you never put off loving me. I know that my obsessive-compulsive personality made it difficult for you, but it was you who taught me to live life to the fullest, enjoy the present, and trust that tomorrow would take care of itself.

This story is about a woman who put off doing something that she wanted to do for 30 years. She waited until the time was right for her to do it and more importantly, when it mattered the most to her. This is an incredible story about a courageous woman and just another reason why the hospice care center was a vital resource for healing, love, and hope. As I entered the room, several people were holding hands across the bed. A beautiful ruby red crucifix lay neatly across the patient's chest. It glistened against her fair skin and the pale pink hospital gown. I assumed she was the mother. A younger woman was sitting on the right side of the bed and an older man was seated on the left. They were leaning over the bed, each one holding the woman's hands. It looked like a bridge of love connected by their touch. I said, "Hello, I'm Susan, a volunteer. I didn't mean to disturb you. May I get you anything?" "No, they said in unison, we are fine." I said, "Your cross is magnificent." The woman smiled and said, "The cross is a gift from my daughter. I did something very special today. Would you like to know what I did?" "Absolutely," I responded. The daughter said, "My mom converted to Catholicism at the center today. She finally did the deed." The daughter got very emotional and started to cry. The husband said, "We're all together now in body, spirit, and our faith." The man started to cry, the mother fell apart, and I grabbed the box of tissues and joined in.

The woman squeezed their hands a little harder. She said, "It took me 30 years to finally make this decision. I was raised a Lutheran. My husband was brought up Roman Catholic and that's the way we raised our daughter. She became a Eucharist minister with her church five years ago. My three grandchildren are Catholic. My daughter and husband wanted me to convert, but they never pressured me. They wanted it to be my own choice. Two years ago I was diagnosed with ovarian cancer. I spent all my time going to doctors, having treatments, and dealing with an illness that continued to get worse. The time went by so quickly. It wasn't until I came into the center that I realized I didn't have very much of it left. Facing my death was all the incentive I needed to finally finish up that unfinished business. My daughter flew here and contacted a friend who was a local priest. They rushed the paper work through and now I am a full-bodied Roman Catholic. I know that my conversion made my daughter and husband happy, but I had to do this for myself. We are a family complete in every sense of the word. I am glad that I still had the time left. It really is never too late for some things." I said, "It's an honor for hospice to have been able to share this wonderful experience with you. Congratulations on your completion of an incredible journey."

The daughter said that she wanted to get a cup of coffee. I asked if I could go with her. As we were walking she said, "I'm not questioning my belief in God or the power of my faith, but why did this have to happen? This is my mother and she is too young to die. What good could really come out of something so terribly wrong? It's not right and it doesn't make any sense." I said, "Your mother converted to Catholicism after 30 years. That is something good." The daughter's eyes welled up with tears. She said, "I know that in my heart, but it's too painful to think about loosing her. I only feel her pain and see her suffering. I know in time that I'll appreciate this experience that the three of us have shared. Yes, we completed a 30-year journey together while there was still time to make something good happen." We said good night. As she walked away she said, "I am very thankful for the precious gift of time."

On the way home, I thought about the experience I had shared with this family. What had the most impact on me what the fact that this woman was true to herself. She converted when she was ready to and even though her conversion brought comfort and joy to her family, she had to do it when the timing was right for her. She was fortunate to still have the time to be able to share this experience with her family. Therefore, it is never too late to complete something you've been postponing or avoided doing. It is never too late to take a chance and risk it all to find the fulfillment of a lifetime. It is never too late to make a dream come true. It is never too late to make someone happy or to be true to yourself. It is never too late to find that inner peace. However, it is too late to do all of those things and do you know when it is? It is too late after you have taken your last breath. When the dying process is complete, it is too late. Until that final moment of life, there is still time to make a change, fulfill a dream, or complete that unfinished business.

We have all delayed, postponed, or "shelved" something that wasn't important. And there's absolutely nothing wrong in putting some things off. There always seems to be so much time ahead of us. It's easy to think that our personal book of life will be open forever and that our pages are endless. It's natural to say, "I'll do it later, I have no time for this now. It's not convenient and I have other more important matters to deal with. I'll get to it eventually and there's always tomorrow." However, we all know that in our heart of hearts one-day we will run out of tomorrows. But, there's no law that says everything has to be done on schedule. Priorities change according to the times, the needs of the person, and the different stages in their life. When you first thought about doing something perhaps it didn't matter as much as it might in the future. The same issue later on might become more significant, meaningful, or even necessary.

If you knew in advance how many days you had left, would you conduct your life differently? What would your priorities be? What would you do if the issue was important to someone else? Does putting something off matter any more or less when it involves someone that you love? What happens when your choices and decisions not only affect your life but the lives of your loved ones? How much can you compromise when it involves the people that you care about the most? Is it more important to please others rather than to please yourself? If what you do isn't for the right reasons, might you feel guilty or angry afterwards? These are a few of the questions you might have to ask yourself before making an important decision now or in the future. Since you don't know how long you have, it is important to understand that the choices you make today will effect your tomorrows. However, what is most important is for you to be the one to determine when the timing is right for you to do what you want to do. You must be true to yourself and have peace of mind when you make those important decisions.

Looking back now, the little things that seemed so important were not. It didn't matter who took out the trash, as long as it got done. It didn't matter who did the laundry as long as our clothes were clean. What did matter was the quality of our life and the way we lived it. You once said to me, "Susan, sometimes life doesn't make any sense and it doesn't have to. Why do you have to question adversity? Why not accept it and learn from it? Remember that something good always comes out of something terrible. It just may happen at another time. It may take a while before you understand why something happened the way it did because things aren't always the way they seem. One day what was unclear might become very obvious." You were so smart about life, living, and never put off the important things in life. We completed almost everything we had to do before your death and we tied up our loose ends. We felt completion in a life well lived and a love worth investing in. I am glad that we never put off the one most important thing. We never put off saying, "I love you."

I'll say so long for a little while.

I love you.

Susan

And I Held Their Hands With A Hospice Heart

Chapter 19

A Wife Who Had To Talk To Her Sister About Dying Because Her Husband Could Not Deal With It And She Didn't Understand Why It Was So Hard That They Couldn't

"If we talk about living, then we must talk about dying. Both go hand in hand. Denying it will not prevent it"

December 1999

Dear Jeff,

Death doesn't take a vacation or have a day of rest. The Christmas and New Year's Holidays are next week and though it's been 5 years since your death, they are still horribly painful. I find it difficult to stay positive and keep myself together. I disliked these holidays when you were alive and I detest them even more now that you are gone. Getting together with family and friends, shopping for gifts wrapped in pretty red and green paper, lights twinkling as they decorate houses and shrubs, and music telling of joy and salvation only seems hypocritical and sacrilegious. The focus is on partying and celebrating, yet all I hear is noise and what I feel is chaos and disruption. I find comfort knowing that these days will soon be over. I've learned to celebrate every day and I am thankful for the gift of life. I'll spend more time at the care center and give to those in need. My problems compared to theirs are small and insignificant. Many will loose their loved ones. Their holidays in the future will become saddening and heartbreaking times. They will not feel joyous or want to celebrate because their loved ones are gone forever. Their pain and sorrow will be too much for them to bear. Many will be unable to talk openly about those who have died. Some will pretend by avoiding or denying their loss. Loneliness and despair will become their family while isolation and depression their bedmates. The subject of death and dying can make holidays even more unbearable.

But, why are the issues of death and dying so difficult to talk about? Why can't death be discussed as easily as birth, love, health, and happiness? Why aren't these topics openly and comfortably dealt with in schools, at home, or between friends? Is it fear or denial that causes most people to wait until they are faced with their own mortality or a loved one's impending death to speak about it? And why are we able to talk about death when it pertains to a business or if it is in a religious setting? But why are we unable to verbalize it in or at an intimate and personal level? And why do we mislead so many children about the issue of death shielding them from the truth? If death is the eventuality of life, why is this subject not discussed as part of the educational curriculum? Would it make it easier to talk about death and/or dying if perhaps one was more comfortable with his or her own mortality? And why does death have to be a depressing topic of conversation? Might that indicate that you yourself are a depressing individual or a morbid person? It is a difficult topic to discuss simply for one reason. It is the most personal topic you may ever have to think about. Yes, it is a serious matter. But maybe, just maybe isn't there a possibility that by having an open conversation about this subject might lessen the feeling of gloom and doom that does accompany this eventual reality.

This story tells about a woman who couldn't talk to her husband about her death. She turned to her twin sister for comfort and support instead of her spouse of 30 years. He couldn't talk about it because it was too painful for him to accept. This story did not happen at the care center but in an airport terminal while I was flying to New York to visit my parents. As I placed my bag under my seat, I glanced at the woman sitting to the right of me. She was small, terribly thin, and looked lost in her seat. Since we were seated in an emergency exit row, my first thought was that she wouldn't be able to open up the door in case of an emergency. About an hour later, I realized that she hadn't moved. She never uncrossed her legs, moved around in her seat, or turned the pages of the driver's manual she was totally engrossed in. She just continued to read as if it was the last book she might ever pick up. I finally said to her, "You are so intense in that driver's handbook. Either that's the most interesting book about motoring you've ever read or there is something hidden behind those unturned pages."

She laughed. Her face lit up with the most beautiful smile I'd ever seen. She said, "I've been driving for 40 years in Chicago. I recently moved to South Carolina and I have to take a driver's test. Is it that different driving a car in Illinois? I wonder what I've been doing wrong." I said, "They want you to feel like you're sweet-sixteen again. Pretend it's your first time behind the wheel and make it fun." She said, "I'll put the peddle to the floor and take the instructor for a ride they'll never forget." She noticed the red hospice heart pin on my jacket and said, "Are you involved with hospice?" "Yes, I said. I volunteer at a care center in Boca Raton, Florida. I've been involved with hospice since my husband's death 5 years ago." She said, "When my twin sister in Ohio died two years ago, hospice came into her home and took care of everything. The saddest thing was that my sister couldn't talk about her death with her husband. He was in complete denial and wouldn't allow her to talk about it either. He would leave the room when she brought the subject up. My sister and I were always close. She called me several times a day to talk about her feelings. At first, she'd cry. Then she would calm down and feel better. She said that she wasn't afraid of dying. She just needed to talk with someone close to her. I was glad that I could help her through this. She understood that he was suffering in his own way, but in 30 years this was the first time they couldn't talk about something. Her frustrations were as painful as the physical aspects of her disease and she got very depressed. He was the one that she was the closest to and now he wasn't there for her. I don't understand why he couldn't talk to her."

I said, "I hear this all the time. Some people are afraid to talk about death and wait until it's too late. After their loved one has died, they have feelings of guilt because they hadn't done something that mattered to the deceased. People who are able to discuss both their illness and their death are more at peace with their loved ones. It was wonderful that you were there for your sister. How is her husband doing?" She said, "He called me a month after her death. His feelings of guilt were overwhelming. He felt lost and knew that he had failed her when she needed him the most. It took several months of professional counseling, but he is better now. He realized that he should have talked to her and that he missed this opportunity to help her. He loved her so much and dealt with the situation the way he had to. He couldn't bring himself to acknowledge her death because he didn't want to be without her. Now, he talks to me about her death and his own mortality. He doesn't feel guilty any more. We are closer than we have ever been and we know that my sister was loved by the two of us." Our conversation was over and so was the plane trip. We collected our things and were thankful that her driver's manual and my hospice heart brought us together.

As previously stated, why is the subject of death so difficult to talk about? Why isn't it appropriate to discuss around the dinner table, the office, or at a social event? Why does it have to be scary, secretive, and unmentionable? Why are some people so afraid of it?

Perhaps it's the fear of the unknown and its just human nature to run away from the things we know so little about. Perhaps death's mysteries are frightening because no one has ever come back to tell us what it was like? Or have they? Death is only frightening if frightening is what you want it to be. Why not take those fears and grow through them by helping others and discussing these issues openly and honestly. We talk about dying when we set up our financial portfolios, for estate planning, or when we purchase health and life insurance policies. We want our families to be financially safe and secure in case we die. Why should we wait until the very end to say to our family, "I want to talk to you about my death, because I want you to inherit my deepest feelings and concerns as well as my material estate?"

My father was a man who read the obituary column first thing in the morning. He wanted to see who was in it, but he always said that he wasn't ready to see his name in print. He was glad that he wasn't mentioned for he wanted to live forever. My parents never felt comfortable discussing death with me even as a young child when I found my grandmother and several other relatives dead in their beds. No one ever talked about their passing with me. And why didn't they? Might it have made it easier for me to understand what I would have to face in the future? Why wouldn't my parents tell me the truth and help a little girl to understand what living and dying was about. It was my confusion about death and dying that I think caused me more uncertainty and problems later on. Maybe talking about death would have been the only thing that made any sense, because it was the only thing that they could have done. Talking about your feelings while you are still alive and able to do it makes sense because doing that can be a great source of comfort and peace to those you leave behind. It might become more difficult after you or your loved one has gone. Circumstances might make it impossible to be able to share your feelings with someone you love, because everyone involved has their own emotional agenda and needs. Everyone deals with loss his or her own way.

If you're loved ones can't help you through this time, then talk to someone who can because sharing your feelings is critically important. My husband knew that he was going to die, but he didn't want to talk about it. He only mentioned it once during those two years and then it was to tell me that he wanted to be cremated. Though I shared the physical, mental, and emotional aspects of his death, I didn't share his spiritual concerns. I am sorry for that, because I missed out on something that was very important to me. I could have tried harder to get him to talk to me, but I respected his feelings even though I had the need to know for myself how he really felt. Maybe he couldn't accept the fact that he was dying. Maybe he thought that it wouldn't happen if he didn't talk about it. Maybe it was just too painful. Maybe he was at peace with himself and didn't have the need to share his feelings. In the end, it was his life and it was up to him to bring this matter up. I never knew how he felt about his death, but I knew how much he loved his life.

I'll say so long for a little while.

I love you.

Susan

Chapter 20

This Man Thought That He Was In Control Of His Emotions After His Mother Died But He Had Not Taken The Necessary Time To Grieve And His Emotional Waves Finally Caught Up With Him

"Learning through the recovery process means taking back control back of your life."

January 2000

Dear Jeff,

For 25 years, we celebrated two joyous occasions together in January. One was on January 11th when we were married and the other, your birthday on January 17th. I remember those wonderful days in my mind, but I try not to feel them in my heart. This still remains a painful time for me. I stay busy and focus on other things and I'm thankful when the week is over. You were a gentleman and a gentle man. I never told you before how much I envied your discipline and self-control. I loved your wonderful disposition. You were even tempered, hated arguments, confrontations, and loud conversation. You listened carefully to people before choosing the appropriate words and respected other's opinions though you might not have agreed with them. We certainly had different personalities. I was argumentative, bossy, mean, short tempered, and liked confronting everything head on. I pushed people's buttons to get them to react and I reacted instinctively instead of waiting for the proper time. I know that it was my own frustrations and disappointments that fueled many of our arguments and that my volatile temper, moodiness, and anger came from my personal unresolved issues.

My writing has allowed me to express my most intimate feelings in a healthy way. It has become both my best friend and my therapy. When I looked up the meaning of the word emotion, it stated that it was a noun that meant strong feelings. It's a complex and usually strong subjective response to a particular feeling like love or hate. Synonyms include affection, sentiment, passion, and sympathy. Since your death, I've learned a lot about myself. I realized that feeling emotional and acting emotionally are two very different things. I'm trying to become a better listener and to think before I speak. I'm trying not to put myself into compromising situations that will drain my energy and take from me what I do not have. I'm trying to deal only with what I know I can handle and I'm trying not to control the things that are out of my control. Being on my own has taught me that I'm the one who's accountable and responsible for everything I do. I can not blame anyone or make any excuses for something if it doesn't work out. I've gotten stronger emotionally and gained more confidence in myself by facing myself.

The following story is personal because it involved a close friend. The issue deals with the complex vulnerability of one's emotional state after a loved one's death. It was 7:00 AM when the phone rang. His voice was wavering and I didn't know if he was laughing or crying. I said, "Slow down. Take a deep breath. What's the matter?" He said, "I thought that I was handling things but I'm not. My mind is racing. I didn't sleep last night and I can't get myself under control. I can't stop crying. I haven't been this way since Mom died." I said, "It's only been two months since her death. You are still in shock and dealing with her loss. It's natural to be upset. Do you want me to come over?" "Yes, he said. I'd like that" An hour later, I knocked on his door. When he answered, he looked exhausted and dazed. His eyes stared through me, not at me. I gave him a hug and said, "We'll have a pot of caffeine and a good cry. What a great way to start the day." His beautiful smile turned to laughter. His wonderful laugh then turned to tears.

He said, "Mom was ill with emphysema for five years. During this time, I did everything I could to give quality to her life. She was my best friend. My life revolved around her. I was able to adapt and adjust to the different stages of her illness and I could usually predict what was going to happen next and how I might react. But I didn't realize until now what a serious toll her death had taken on me. These past 2 months have been horrible and I'm exhausted. I feel alone, abandoned, and afraid. I feel like my purpose for living is gone. I don't know what to expect or when I'll loose control." I said, "I admired your devotion to your mother. You never complained or stopped trying to give her the very best. Even when you were worn out and overwhelmingly grieved, you never said that you couldn't take it any longer. You were always able to handle everything." He said, "Your husband died after a long illness so you know how difficult it is watching someone you love die. For 5 years, I made her illness and well being my priority. I knew that she was dying, but I still had her in my life.

I didn't take on any other responsibilities during her last few months. I asked friends and hospice for help when I needed it. I tried to keep my life as orderly and organized as possible and I conserved my emotional energy. But I had to handle the funeral arrangements, her personal affairs, and everything else. I thought that I was doing all right until now. I'm not coping well and I'm questioning my emotional stability." I said, "What happened that made you feel like this? Something unexpected caught you off guard and made you react this way." He said, "I was cleaning out my freezer a week ago. There was a container of homemade chicken soup that I was going to bring to mom. I went to remove it and it fell to the floor splattering over everything. I got hysterical and fell to my knees crying like a baby. It took me four hours to compose myself. I stayed in bed for two days. Yesterday, I was in the market. One of mom's favorite songs was playing. I lost control again and ran from the store. I had to pull off the road because I was crying so hard.

When mom was alive, I was able to deal with my ups and downs better because I could focus on her and her illness. Now, I feel emotionally caught off guard and unprepared. I feel vulnerable and unsure of my emotions. I don't know what will get to me or how I will react. I don't know when I'm going to loose control or for how long. I'm frightened because I don't have any signs or signals warning me of my instability. I feel like I'm setting myself up for problems and I don't know what to do. I'm scared because I don't know how to deal with this unexpected emotional turmoil." I said, "It's going to take a long time for you to know what you can deal with and what you can't. Live each day, conserve your energy, and don't waste it on anything that you know you can not handle. Try not to set yourself up. As time goes along, you'll get better at doing this. The grieving and healing process is a slow one. Take the time to let the time take care of you." We spoke many times in the days and weeks that followed. He shared his feelings, dealt with his emotions, and faced every situation as it came along. He continued to do what he always had done. He lived.

Critical times that involve a life-threatening illness don't follow a set of rules. You may not realize how emotionally exhausted and drained you are because your energies and focus were centered on someone else. However, after your loved one's death, the caregiver's emotional stability has been seriously tested and compromised. Once the grieving and healing process has begun, your reactions might be different than they were before because the situation has changed. Your loved one is gone and you are back focussing on your life. Your actions and reactions revolve again around yourself. This is the time when you'll start to experience what I call "emotional waves." Some waves will be gentle and others violent. Their intensity will depend on timing and your vulnerability. Sometimes you'll think that you "have it all together." You're feeling emotionally in control, more stable, and secure. You're proud of the progress you've made in handling your loss. These "gentle emotional waves" make you feel peaceful and calm. They are reassuring and supporting. They help you to remember the feelings of love and happiness.

However, sometimes without warning, something unexpected will happen and a spontaneous emotional reaction will be triggered. Instantly, you'll feel out of control, fragile, and vulnerable again. The gentle emotional waves have now become stormy, rough, and upsetting. These are "violent emotional waves" that are strong and powerful. They'll catch you off guard and they won't care where or when. They'll come crashing against your heart and they will tear at your soul. You'll feel pain, disorder, and confusion. It might be a song, a picture, a smell, a phrase, or one of a thousand different things, but something will happen that will remind you of your loved one. Something will get to your raw open vulnerability. The pain and anguish you'll experience will make you feel as though your loss happened for the very first time. You will not be able to control or stop that emotional rush of violent waves as your feelings come pouring out.

When it comes to taking back the emotional control of your life, there is no time limit. There is no way to predict how long your healing process will take because dealing with your grief and loss is both personal and private. Until you are faced with this situation, you will not know how you are going to handle it. How you think that you will cope and how you actually do cope can not be determined. But, whether your life experiences are good or bad, you will react because everyone has feelings and emotions. Each one of us has an inherent emotional component. Feelings can not be taught and emotions can not be forced on anyone. You may choose to deal with your emotions privately. You might need to talk with someone about your feelings. You might guard your feelings carefully because you won't trust your emotions to anyone else. Perhaps your grief will be too painful to share. Maybe you will begin to act them out, at first upon yourself, then perhaps on others. You might think that you are emotionally back in control and ready to handle any situation that might arise. However, the emotional rollercoaster ride that accompanies a loved one's death can catch you off guard. In time, you will learn how to deal with your "emotional waves" and you'll let them take you wherever they will. You'll get better at coping with them and you will grow through them. You will get better at understanding yourself and you will become the master of your emotions again. Remember that time is the greatest gift of all. Thank you Jeff for your 25 years of time.

I'll say so long for a little while.

I love you.

Susan

Chapter 21

The Effects Of A Long Term Illness Can Be Difficult For The Entire Family And For This Woman She Didn't Want To Be A Burden To The Ones She Loved Any Longer

"Carry the burdens of life proudly on your shoulders."

February 2000

Dear Jeff,

Valentine's Day is next week. Everywhere I go there are displays with heart shaped boxes of candy, bouquets of flowers, red wrapped packages, and cards that say, "I love you." Thirty-one years ago on February 14th, 1969, you gave me my first Valentine's Day box of candy. I came home early from work to make you a special dinner. When I went into the bedroom to change, lying on my pillow was a heart shaped box wrapped in gold and red foil. One yellow rose and a card lay next to it. I read your card and started to cry. You had written the most loving inscription I'd ever read. I opened my gift and there were two pounds of assorted

Godiva truffles. I said to myself, "I'm only going to have one piece. Then I'll make dinner." Unfortunately, I couldn't stop eating them and before I knew it I had devoured a dozen delicious pieces of chocolate. When you came home, I was in the bathroom throwing up. I'd made myself ill and spent the remainder of the evening in bed. You ordered a pizza and ate by yourself in the kitchen. I heard you laughing about it all night, but I was too sick to care. The following year you asked me if I wanted another box of candy. I said, "Please gift wrap one Hershey Bar and a $20.00 bill." We shared the candy bar, spent the money on pizza and wine, and celebrated in bed. Thank you for sharing 25 wonderful Valentine's Days with me.

I was going to visit my parents tomorrow. Mom turned 88 and Dad is 89. Though they're still doing well, the aging process is a long, slow, and difficult one. It's been bittersweet for me to watch what has happened to them. At some time during my visit, the subject of independent and assisted living would always come up. Dad would say, "One day I just won't wake up. I'm going to die in my sleep." I'd say, "Dad, that's what you'd like, but you know that's not what usually happens." Mom would be adamant and never wavered in her beliefs. She would say, "Dad and I will maintain our apartment, take care of ourselves, and we'll never be a burden to anyone. When the time comes, I don't want my children to give up their lives for us. You have your own responsibilities to take care of. Parents must be on their own no matter how difficult it is for their children. The best intentions aren't always for the best." I'd say to Mom, "I love you and Dad and I'll do anything I can to make your life better. How can loving you and wanting to take care of you be a burden to me?" My mother would refuse to discuss it any longer and the issue would be put on hold until the next visit.

This story is about a woman who didn't want to be a burden to her family. As she faced her own mortality, she told me what the meaning of the word "burden" meant from a patient's point of view. She explained why she didn't want her family to make her their responsibility any longer. Our conversation would change the way I felt about this issue and it helped me to understand why my mother felt the way that she did. The woman had been a patient at the care center for several weeks. Whenever I'd go into her room, there were always lots of people visiting her. Everyone would be eating, talking or laughing and the atmosphere was upbeat and positive. There was also the longest piece of plastic oxygen tubing hanging on the floor, coiled under the chair, and running over the sheets. When I went in last night, she was alone and watching CNN. I said, "Hi. I'm Susan, a volunteer. I feel like this is the first time we've been formally introduced. You've always had a lot of company visiting and we've never gotten a chance to talk. Is there anything exciting going on in the world today?" "No, she smiled and said, but I'm going to a nursing home tomorrow. Now that's something worth talking about."

I said, "Besides all the company, do you know what I've noticed the most?" "What," she responded. I said, "I've never seen anyone with an oxygen line as long as yours. You could strangle yourself with the extra 50 feet of plastic tubing. Your nurses must be pretty sure that you aren't going to hang yourself from the sprinkler head on the ceiling." She started to laugh and needed to catch her breath. A few minutes later she said, "If laughter is the best medicine then I feel great. I've noticed something about you, too. When you've come into my room you always look happy and you wear colorful clothes." "Thank you, I said. Would you like some company? I'd like to know why you're going to the nursing home tomorrow." "Yes, she said, just let me untangle myself first." I raised the bed and propped her up against a couple of pillows. I curled up at the foot of the bed half leaning over her legs. She took a sip of water and tugged gently on her oxygen line. She said, "It's still pumping air just like me." I said, "If someone comes in and sees us all knotted up in your plastic tubing, it won't look good for hospice." She laughed again and said, "Disruptive. That's the word that describes my life and everyone else's now. Disruptive. We don't need any more disruptions.

I'm 69 years old. I've been divorced for 25 years and my son lives near by. I've worked my entire life doing what I call blue-collar jobs. I love people, but I like being independent and taking care of myself. I've maintained my home, a beautiful garden, and I love playing cards, especially poker. Many of my visitors are poker buddies. Five years ago, I was diagnosed with lung cancer and emphysema. I've suffered for 4 ½ years with this disease, but the past 6 months have been hell. The cancer has spread throughout my body and I'm requiring more and more assistance. My son and daughter-in-law want me to live with them. They just built a home and set up a beautiful room for me. But, my son works from 7 AM to 7 PM six days a week. My daughter-in-law has been wonderful, but she has enough responsibility taking care of their 2-year old little girl. I'm at a point where I need a full-time nurse and constant supervision. Can you imagine what it's like having to ask your grand daughter to get you something? They want to take care of me all the time. They want to do everything for me." He says, "Mom, you've never been a burden and never will be."

She continued, "Because he loves me so much and wants to help, he thinks he knows what's best for me. He doesn't understand that this isn't an issue about love. It's an issue about choice and respecting someone else's wishes. I can't put them through anymore. I'm not their child and they aren't my parents. I've disrupted, changed, and rearranged their lives long enough. Long-term illnesses don't just affect the patient. They take a serious toll on everyone involved. It's time for them to stop taking care of me and to come and visit me. They can love me as their mother but they must let me go as a friend. I do not want any further disruptions in my life or theirs. I knew that hospice would help me when the time came. Well, the time has come." I said, "You still never specifically told me why you're going to a nursing home tomorrow. Why don't you stay here at the center?" She said, "I can have hospice help where ever I am. My illness could go on for a while and I want to have people to talk with. I want to be with people like me. Maybe I'll get a roommate who doesn't need a diaper and who can play poker. Tomorrow will be another adventure."

My eyes welled up with tears. I reached for the tissues and said, "I've been dealing with this issue and my parents for several years. They are nearing 90 and are beginning to require more assistance. They aren't dealing with anything life threatening, but the aging process has caught up with them. It's becoming more difficult for them to take care of themselves. I want to be with them all the time and take care of them. They are my responsibility and it's my duty as their child." "No, she said. You can not take care of them. You can help them and you can make their transitions easier, but you must respect the fact that they want to maintain their independence and continue making their own choices. You have to step back and look at the situation from both sides." I said, "Thank you for talking to me about this. You've helped me to understand my parents' beliefs and to respect their wishes." I kissed her forehead and said goodnight. As I stood outside her room, I thought about how perceptive this woman was. She knew what was best for her and what she wanted for her family. She helped me to realize that I'd been dealing with this issue as a child who one day might become a caregiver. When she used the word disruptive to describe this time in her life, she changed my perception and interpretation of the meaning of the word burden forever.

There's a big difference between taking care and giving care to someone. It's easy to love someone so much that you think you know what's best for them. But, what you think is best might not be what's best. What is important is that you allow the individual to decide what they feel is best for them. It's their decision, not yours. Understanding this issue from both perspectives may not make it any easier to deal with, but everyone involved must honestly and openly be able to express their feelings. I know now what my mother meant when she said that she didn't want to be a burden to her children. In the future, when this issue comes up, I'll give Mom a hug and say, "You have never been and never will be a burden, but it's up to you to decide what is best for you. Even if I don't agree with you, I will respect your decision." Jeff, you were never a burden to me and I hope you never felt like one either. You were my husband and my best friend. I took care of you because I loved you. Maybe as husband and wife we looked at the issue of being a burden differently than our parents did. But, I'd like to think that when we said, "I do until death do us part," those vows removed the word burden from our marriage vocabulary.

Happy Valentine's Day

I'll say so long for a little while.

I love you.

Susan

Chapter 22

This Woman Felt That She Caused Her Husband's Illness And Was Responsible For Everything But Her Feelings Of Guilt And Anger Didn't Do Any Good Nor Could It Change Anything

"Illnesses happen but diseases are spread."

March 2000

Dear Jeff,

We met in the 5th grade when I walked by you and you said, "I like your Bobby socks." Our relationship continued to go and grow for 36 more years. Throughout high school, college, and into our married life, it was our ability to communicate, laugh, and have fun that kept us together. We simply understood and accepted each other. When I was being stubborn, moody, and causing trouble, this made you laugh. When I told you that I hated school, authority, and taking orders, you called that independence. When I irritated and provoked people, you found my behavior interesting and unique. When I was 16 and ran away from home you said I was adventurous. When I told you that I hated my life, you listened. You said, "Susan, your terrible behavior is because you're angry, frustrated, and disappointed. You're a young girl trapped in an adult's mind and dreams. It would be easier to harness the wind than to try and control you." You liked me, saw my potential, and I loved you for that. My disruptive antics may have given my family much aggravation and many sleepless nights, but thankfully, it never made them seriously ill. You and I had such different personalities. You never wanted to cause any disturbances or problems. You hated arguments, confrontations, turmoil, and wouldn't have harmed another human being. Yet, it was you who ended up hurting those you loved and those who loved you the most.

How much guilt does someone have to have to get them to believe that they were capable of willing someone into getting sick? Is this self-emotional mutilation a form of punishment for not being able to deal with their own unresolved issues? Why would anyone want to mentally torture themselves by thinking this way? Are their feelings too painful to acknowledge and even more unbearable to deal with? Are their emotional conflicts so deeply buried within their own being that they fail to notice their own red flags and warning signals along the way? Could something ignite their feelings and put them on a collision course with the truth and themselves? Could something happen causing an explosion of rage, anger, blame and guilt so out of control that it was impossible to stop? This story is about a woman who blamed herself for her husband's worsening medical condition and how her feelings of guilt and anger nearly cost her whatever time she had left with him.

The care center was quiet last night. I watched as a woman wandered nervously around the waiting area. She reminded me of a caged animal pacing back and forth anxiously anticipating something to happen. I went over and said, "My name is Susan. I'm a volunteer. Is there anything I can get you?" Her stare was cold and blank. She peered through me seemingly unaware of my presence or what I'd said. Moments later she said, "I brought my husband into the center tonight and it's all my fault. I thought that I was prepared for this, but I'm not. I never thought that I could feel such rage. I want to explode and take everyone with me." She started to cry and her body was heaving and shaking uncontrollably. She was emotionally exhausted. I said, "Please sit down with me. The nurses are tending to your husband. They'll come and get you in a little while. Take this time for yourself. If you don't get yourself together, you won't be able to help your husband." She fell into the couch crying hysterically. She was overwhelmed and needed to talk to someone. I said, "My husband was ill for a long time, too. I can emphasize with your sadness and frustration. It's difficult to see your husband here. If you want to be alone, I understand. But, if you want to yell, scream, punch, or kick me, I can take it. I like a good smack once in a while. Just do it!" She burst out laughing and said, "I don't want to hit you but I might throw myself in front of a train."

I said, "Would you like to talk about it? I've got time and I'd like to be here for you now. The center is a good place to talk about your feelings." She said, "This is my fault. I did this to him. I hate myself for it. I can't control my anger any longer. I pressured my husband into moving to Florida. I was a teacher and he was an accountant. He loved his work. I'd been nagging him for years to leave New York, buy a smaller home, and move where it was warmer. I wanted a different life while we could still have it. We're both 58 years old. Our two children are grown and have their own families. After 30 years, we sold our beautiful house, left our jobs, our family and friends." She started crying again and walked away.

A few minutes later she came back and said, "We moved here 6 months ago. He only made this move to make me happy. My husband's had Parkinson's disease for 4 years. He's done very well and the disease has progressed slowly. He's also had chronic ulcerative colitis for years. Sometimes his attacks were debilitating but he always got better and most of the time he did whatever he wanted to do. We trusted his doctors and he always got the best care.

When I look back now, I realize that he was getting worse. I should have seen the warning signals he was giving me. I was selfish and didn't want to notice what was happening to him. We should have stayed there. I should have known better. When we moved into the new house, we didn't know the area or anyone in it. We didn't know anything. We never asked our physicians in New York to refer him to a local doctor. I thought we'd do that once we got settled in. We were in our home for one month when he had an acute ulcerative colitis attack. He was rushed to the hospital hemorrhaging in critical condition. Within 2 weeks his Parkinson's worsened. One week later he developed pancreatitis. Now he was too ill to take up north. We went to several doctors, different hospitals, 2 rehab centers, and now hospice. I made all the wrong choices about everything. Why didn't I want to see it? Six months ago I moved here looking for a new life. This was not what I'd expected." She couldn't control her anger and stormed out into the courtyard. She kicked and punched a tree several times until she had no energy left. She leaned against the bark weeping from exhaustion.

I didn't go after her as I thought she needed to be alone. When she came in she said, "It's my guilt that's killing me." I said, "Why is your husband in the hospice program?" She said, "His pain was excruciating and his doctors couldn't stabilize him. He was bleeding rectally and his pancreatitis wouldn't improve. He couldn't eat or drink and lost 35 pounds within weeks. He couldn't control his movements or get up. The doctors said they couldn't do anything else and recommended hospice. Everything happened so quickly. All I want now is to take him home. That's what he wants, too." I said, "You made the choices that you thought were best at the time. Hindsight doesn't work and the guilt will destroy you. Focus all your energy and attention now on your husband while you still have some time. Make him your priority and please forgive me for saying this, but your husband could have said NO. You didn't cause your husband's illnesses and you didn't put him here. I hope that you'll be kinder to yourself." She said, "I have other issues that I've never dealt with and many reasons to feel guilty. I'll try to focus on my husband and we'll get back into our new home. That's what we both need. It's going to take me a long time to honestly face myself and deal with my unfinished emotional business." With that, the nurse came and told her that she could see her husband now. She thanked me and said goodnight. Her husband went home a week later.

Many people want to blame their problems on someone or something else. When things don't turn out the way they'd wanted them to or if the results aren't what they'd expected, why not make somebody else responsible for the failure? It feels good to take the responsibility off your shoulders and place it on somebody else's. But, feeling responsible and being responsible are different matters. This woman didn't want to blame anybody else but herself for her problems. She wanted to be responsible for everything bad that had happened, including her husband's condition. Using phrases like "should have," "could have," and "would have" only reinforced how negative and guilty she felt about herself and her decisions. Her husband's medical crisis helped to bring out unresolved past issues that she hadn't wanted to deal with. Unless she rids herself of this self-emotional mutilation, she will never be happy. She must now spend the remaining time with her husband and make things better for the both of them. She'll never know if this might have happened even if they hadn't moved, because this might have been an unfortunate coincidence.

You can give someone a headache, an ulcer, or high blood pressure, but you can't give another person cancer, heart disease or diabetes. You can develop a medical problem because of diet, lifestyle, and stress, but you can't think someone into developing a life-threatening illness. You can cause suffering and bring pain to someone, but you can't will a person into an illness or death. As in our case, someone did give you a sexually transmitted disease and it was the HIV virus and AIDS that took your life. But, it still was the disease that killed you and not the person. I could have blamed you so many times for your death because of your promiscuity but I could not save you from it. The only thing I could do was make a choice and that choice saved my life. You allowed this virus into your body but I did not allow it into mine. To this day I will not take the guilt upon myself that I had in any way been responsible for what happened to you. Your life was your responsibility and your death didn't have to happen, but I let you be who you wanted to be and we both had to accept the terrible consequences of those choices.

Being married to you for 25 years and going on without you were both difficult things to do. But, I dealt with your disease and I survived your death. I accept the decisions I've made and I have no regrets. I believe that nothing in life is a mistake and that everything happens for a reason. It just might take a little while to know what that reason is. Five years later, I know that your death opened up a door for me. I didn't know whether to walk through that door or to walk away. I chose to walk through and on the other side of that door was my writing. These stories are the product of your tragic death and the issues I faced have become my therapy. Thank you for opening up a door for me and for giving me the courage and strength to believe in myself.

I'll say so long for a little while.

I love you.

Susan

Chapter 23

This Woman Felt That The Treatment Was Worse Than The Disease And She Chose To Have Quality Of Life Rather Than Suffer Through The Treatments

"Human nature causes us to fight. Instinct drives us to survive. But, the will to live determines how we choose to die."

April 2000

Dear Jeff,

Shortly after we were married, you wanted me to clean your teeth. You came to the VA Hospital where I worked and got into the chair. I put the aspirator in your mouth and started checking your teeth. Five minutes later, you pulled the aspirator from your mouth, jumped up, and left without saying a word. When I got home I asked you why you did that. You said, "I didn't like it. It was uncomfortable. I'm not good at handling pain." I said, "I was checking your teeth and hadn't even started your cleaning. If you think that experience was unpleasant, I hope you never lose any teeth from gum disease." Later that evening you said, "I'm sorry for my childish behavior. I've never been good with doctors and medicine. Can we try again?" A week later, you sat in the chair white knuckled and in a cold sweat, but you had your teeth cleaned. You also made a big production out of taking a pill. I'd watch you stare at it until you got up enough courage to pick it up. Then you placed it on the back of your tongue and threw your head back. I don't know why you didn't choke on it or wrench your neck. I watched you bury them in ice cream and press them into chocolate chip cookies just to get them down. I'm grateful for the first 23 years of our marriage, because you experienced very little discomfort or pain.

Early in 1992, we both knew that you were becoming symptomatic with something serious. Your breathing became labored and you started to snore. It sounded like you were gasping for air. You tired easily and had to stop eating to catch your breath. Your appetite diminished and you lost weight. Your hair started falling out and your skin developed rashes and lesions. You had a dry hacking cough that wouldn't go away. You were once a healthy man who never knew much pain and suffering, but on June 20th, 1992, that would change. Now you were a patient in the hospital fighting for your life. The doctors and the medicines that you had avoided all those years had now become the very things that could save your life. Your body was pricked, jabbed, and punctured several times a day. You inhaled drugs that made you gag. You swallowed dozens of monstrous size pills that made you choke. You had to endure painful treatments and difficult procedures. When the medications and treatments made you violently ill, you continued through this torturous hell. You endured it because you wanted to live. You learned how to become a good patient because you didn't have a choice.

Last night at the care center, I met a woman who decided to stop her treatments because she didn't want to endure any more suffering. She had come to the end of her battle and she wanted to take charge of her life again. Her courage and strength to make that decision reminded me of you. I gathered up my cart and set off down the hall. When I went into her room to bring in some fresh water, I noticed a beautiful quilt draped across the foot of her bed. "Hello, she said, do you have a vodka martini in that pitcher?" I replied, "Did you want olives or a twist of lemon. My name is Susan. I'm your volunteer bartender for the night." "No, she said, plain vodka will be fine." I said, "Other than that martini is there anything else you'd like?" "No, she responded, I'm fine." I said, "That's the most magnificent quilt I've ever seen." Her face lit up. She replied, "I loved making quilts and this one is my favorite. My daughter brought it in. It's been raining all day and my quilt makes me feel warm and cozy." I said, "Would you like some company?" "Yes, she replied, I'd love to bore you with my story."

She said, "I'm 69 years young but I'm 70 years old. I've had emphysema for 5 years, but it wasn't until they found the lung cancer this year that I knew this was it. I had to quit smoking after 50 years. It's the hardest thing I've ever had to do. I went cold turkey 6 months ago and it's been hell. I want one all the time. I also made a decision to give up something else. I stopped my cancer treatments and took myself off all the medications. I was in agony. The treatments were killing me more than the disease. I couldn't eat, swallow, or breathe. I'd rather have no pain and a better quality of life than be at the mercy of the drugs." My eyes welled up with tears. I wasn't prepared for her remarks. It was like reliving your final months all over again. She said the same things that you did when you made your decision to stop your treatments. I said, "I understand what you're saying. My husband was ill for two years. Three months before he died, he said that he couldn't go through any more procedures. He was tired of fighting. He wanted quality of life rather than quantity of days. Whenever I hear this from someone, it always reminds me of him. Would you tell me specifically why you made this decision?" "Yes, she said, I'm not going anywhere in this weather.

Five years ago, I was having difficulty catching my breath. I couldn't walk up stairs, do my housework, and didn't have any energy. The doctor said I had emphysema and told me to quit smoking. He put me on inhalation treatments, oxygen, and medication. I cut back on my physical activity and slowed down. But, I couldn't quit smoking. Last year, I began having sharp stabbing pains up my spine. They weren't consistent and there wasn't any one thing that triggered these violent attacks. When they happened, I was left frozen for hours in the same position. I was afraid to move for fear of another pain. Several doctors and many tests later, a CAT scan showed a large tumor in my left lung. It was inoperable because of the damage from the emphysema. The doctors were bombarding me with facts, statistics, and the different options for treatment. I was so confused and didn't know what to do. When I spoke with my family, everyone agreed that I had to try something. Since the tumor couldn't be surgically removed, I took a chance that chemotherapy and radiation might shrink it. The doctors said that I had a year to live if the treatments worked or I might have 6 months to a year if I did nothing. I said that I'd try anything to stay alive.

I was scheduled for 12 treatments. I was on pain medication and the shooting paralyzing pains in my back had stopped. I was eating again and breathing easier. The first three treatments weren't a problem and I felt fine. But, the fourth one was horrible. I broke out with open cankerous lesions in my mouth, esophagus, and my stomach. The pain was so intense. I couldn't breathe, eat, drink, or swallow. The doctors determined that the radiation wouldn't work. Again I said that I wanted to live and would try chemotherapy. I had one treatment and my blood pressure went soaring. I almost had a stroke. I told my doctors and my family that the treatments were killing me more than the disease. I said that I wanted to spend whatever time I had left without pain, with my family, and that I wanted quality of life. I would rather live 6 months like a human being than to endure a year of unnecessary pain, suffering, and pity. It's my body and my choice. I'll go on the hospice program when the time comes."

I said, "You sound like my husband. He suffered enough from the disease. He didn't need to go through anything else. You are very strong and courageous. I'm thankful that a stormy night and your beautiful quilt that brought us together. I wish you a peaceful night's sleep." She said, "Thank you for coming in. I'm glad that you liked my quilt. Next time however, please bring the Camel's along with the vodka. Good night." I kissed her forehead and left. I stood outside her door and started to cry. She brought up a very emotional and painful issue for me. Just like you, she made a choice. And just like you, she took control back of her life. Her honesty and openness about her decision helped me to understand why you chose to do what you did. She was at peace with herself and her remarkable faith was inspirational. The reasons why people stop their treatments or medications are different. But, the reason why they made this decision remains the same. It's about quality of life and respect for that person's choice to have that quality.

There comes a time in many people's lives when it's time to say I don't want to go through this anymore. You were in the hospital 3 times in 2 years. I watched you endure inhalation treatments that made you cough and choke. You never complained.

I watched vials and vials of blood being taken from your veins. Then I watched your veins collapse. I watched your beautiful body become a human pincushion, but you never complained. We sat in cold sterile hospital rooms and doctor's offices while you waited anxiously for x-rays and tests. I watched you take dozens of pills several times a day hoping that one of them would buy you time and give you some quality. I watched as these toxic drugs poisoned your system making you nauseous and giving you diarrhea. Still you took them and endured their vicious side effects. You never complained. You spent a day in the hospital hoping that a blood transfusion would build your immune system up. I took you home with hick ups that remained with you for 6 weeks until you died. You were too ill then to do anything but cry. I watched as you followed the doctor's instructions doing whatever they told you to do. You did these things without hesitation and I watched you become the best patient any one could become.

I remember the look you gave me in the kitchen that told me you couldn't endure this suffering any longer. With your eyes you told me that you had had enough. You didn't want any more medications, injections, or treatments. You were more miserable than ever. I understood what you wanted to do. You decided to take charge of your life again. You said that this disease wasn't going to rob you of the one thing you'd always had. Quality. You would have quality during your remaining days. You stayed at home, hospice came in and helped, and we stayed together through it all. It was your love for life that enabled you to endure those two years with courage and dignity. I hope that I'll be able to endure the suffering I continue to have as I live my days without you. You give me hope when I have none and strength when I am weak. Thank you.

I'll say so long for a little while.

I love you.

Susan

Chapter 24

A Son Comes To His Father's Deathbed Out Of Respect But It Was Not Because He Loved Him

"I hope you're with your parents having fun."

May 2000

Dear Jeff,

Because of my involvement with hospice, I've seen the many different kinds of relationships that parents and children share. None, however, was more special than the bond you had with your parents. It began when you were adopted at 6 months of age. You were their chosen baby and you fulfilled all their dreams for the next 47 years. I met your parents when I was 11 years old. Even then, you had them eating out of the palm of your hand. It never mattered what you did as long as you were all right. They gave you everything you wanted, but you never took advantage of their generosity. I never heard you say one unkind or harsh word about them. Your relationship went far beyond that of a parent and child.

You respected them, not only because they were your parents, but also because they were honorable and trustworthy people. They adored you and their love went beyond love. They cared about you, not only as their child, but also as a man. They listened whenever you wanted to talk and you listened whenever they wanted to speak. You respected and valued each other's opinions. They were there for you when you wanted their advice, but they never gave it unless you asked for it. The three of you always found the time to be together. I admired the relationship you had with both of them. You were fortunate to have a father and a mother you could talk to. They would have accepted your bi-sexuality or homosexuality because they would have accepted you under any circumstances. They would always have been there for you.

What is the difference between loving, respecting, and honoring your parents? The definition of love means intense affection. Respect means to feel or show deferential regard for something or someone. Honor means esteem, respect, and recognition. Are their meanings so very different? What meanings really separate these words? Aren't they feelings and more importantly aren't they choices? Should love come naturally or should it be a choice? Should you know when you love someone or something because it feels right in your heart? What really is respect? Is it a duty that comes less from the heart and more out of obligation? Is respect something that must be earned? Are you obligated to respect your parents because they are your parents? Do you honor them by recognizing them or do you respect them because you love them? Do you owe your parents anything because you were born? Does birth guarantee that you must love them? Does living dictate that you must respect them? Is parenthood the reason you honor them? Why should you love, respect, or honor your parents when they are dying if you did not do so when they were alive? Why should you treat them any differently in death as you did in life? If they were dying, could you stay away? Could you deny yourself this one last chance to say good bye? If your relationship ended long ago, could you live with your guilt afterwards if you didn't make an attempt to be with them when they died? All these questions pertain to one thing and one thing only. Whether love, respect and honor are feelings or choices it is up to you. You are the only one who knows. You must answer these questions honestly while your parents are alive, because your guilt and torment afterwards could make it even worse.

Last night at the care center, I met a man who had severed the relationship with his father many years ago. When he heard that his father was dying, he had to decide whether to go to his father now or stay away. As I looked down the hallway, he was pulling 2 suitcases. His hair was disheveled, his coat wrinkled, and his shoes made squeaky noises when he walked. He looked like he hadn't slept in days. He stopped in front of me, dropped his bags, and shook his head. He didn't know what to do next. I said, "Hello, my name is Susan. I'm a volunteer. You either need a porter or a cup of coffee." He said, "I just flew in. It was a long flight and I waited hours for a cab. I was told that my father's death was eminent." I said, "Please sign in. We'll find out what room your father's in and I'll take you there. I'm here until 10:00 tonight. Once you've settled down, please come back and have a hot cup of coffee or tea with me."

Fifteen minutes later he was back. He made a cup of coffee and fell into the couch. He said, "I'm not physically tired. I'm mentally exhausted. I've known for several days that he was dying, but I didn't know whether I should come or not. It was a difficult decision to make. I was torn between what was right and what I felt was right. Once I decided to come, I couldn't get here soon enough.

I prayed that I'd get here on time. You might think this is a terrible thing to say, but I didn't come here because I loved my father nor did I respect him. I did it to honor him because he was my father." "No, I said, that's not a terrible thing to say. Other children have said the same thing. I don't think that love, respect, and honor necessarily mean the same thing. What you think is all that matters. You must be true to your heart and do what's right for you. What is important is that you are here and you made it before he passed away. You were fortunate to still have the time." He said, "It was strange talking to him after all these years. I'm not sure if he could even hear me, but I know I did the right thing by coming.

Was I wrong because I wanted a father that I could talk to and share things with? We just never had a good relationship. No matter what I did, he always managed to find fault with it. I never remember him saying anything nice to me. He said that I wasn't good in sports, couldn't play a musical instrument, and that I was an average kid who wouldn't amount to much. I tried so hard to please him, but I could never live up to his expectations. I was a young man with all sorts of issues to deal with and a father who never had the time to talk to me. He kept telling me that I'd have to learn about life just like he had to do. I went to college to please him and lived at home to help my parents out. One day I got tired of the arguments, his negative attitude, and his hateful verbal abuse. I asked him why he never liked me. He said, "Some fathers and sons just don't get along." That's when I left and never looked back. It's been 25 years since we've seen each other. My parents divorced several years later and I keep in touch with my mother.

I'd thought about what to do for days. I finally realized that I didn't have a choice. He was still my father and I had to come. I wouldn't have been able to live with myself afterwards if I hadn't been here. I don't have any resentment or anger towards him for what happened. And, I don't want any guilt later on. He deserves to be honored as my father. I don't love him but I do care." I said, "Would you like me to stay with you? We could sit in the room together." "Yes, he said. Would you do that? I am uncomfortable. He's not a stranger, but in some ways he is." We went into the room and sat down. He never spoke another word to his father who died 2 hours later. He sat with the man who gave him life and was there at his moment of death. The son closed his father's eyes and sat quietly by his side. He said, "Thank you for being here. I feel like I completed something that I needed to do." I said, "You did the right thing. I wish you peace. Good night."

He picked up his bags, walked down the hallway, and left. This was a difficult decision for him to make. It took a lot of courage and compassion for him to come and see his father. He would continue to feel good about himself and the decision he had made, because he was at peace with his father and himself. The past was over and whether he came out of love, respect, or honor it wasn't important. What mattered was that he was with his father when he died. Even when the situation is painful or emotionally disturbing, most children want to be with their dying parents. If it is not possible, whether by choice or circumstance, the child will have to live with the consequences of his or her behavior. If long-standing feelings of guilt are involved, then those problems will probably be made worse after the parents have died. Being with your parents at the time of their death can bring much comfort and peace of mind afterwards. If you answer with your heart, you will always make the right choice. Remember that the past is history and the present is a gift.

I loved your parents because from the time we were married, they accepted me as their daughter. They knew that I loved you. They knew that I would always do the best I could to take care of you. I am thankful because they knew this for 25 years.

They also knew that they weren't loosing a son, but they were gaining a daughter. When you took ill, I didn't know how I was going to tell them. They didn't know about your bi-sexuality. They didn't know about our lifestyle and the difficult decisions we'd made in order to keep our marriage together. Where would I begin? How could I tell them that their perfect child, their adored son had AIDS and could possibly die? How do I prepare them for the horror they were about to face? I called them to the hospital and said, "Mom and Dad, your son, my husband is gravely ill. If he is going to survive, he will need all our love, our energy, and our strength. Together, we can be here for him now because of the incredibly powerful relationship that we've all shared throughout the years."

When they found out about your sexuality, they accepted you as if nothing had changed. That's because nothing had. Your relationship was based on one thing. Love. Unconditional love. You would always be their chosen baby. During your two-year illness, we continued to spend as much time with them as we always had. I remember the beautiful cruise to Bermuda the four of us took. As it was throughout your life, we were with you when you died. They knew that you would have been there for them, too. You would have made certain that no matter where you were or what the circumstances, you would've been at their side. Thank you for loving them, respecting them, and honoring them."

I'll say so long for a little while.

I love you.

Susan

THE END FOR NOW

About the Author

Author • Speaker • Advocate • Philanthropist

Susan Lee Mintz

About the Author

Susan Lee Mintz is a baby-boomer, motivational author, lecturer and fitness guru from Troy, New York. She currently resides in Boca Raton, Florida.

Susan is an HIV/AIDS facilitator for support groups within her area including at her church Jesus People Proclaim International Church in Deerfield Beach, Florida and at Century Village Retirement Community in Boca Raton. She serves as the Executive Director of the "I Love My Life Ministry" and the wellness center at Jesus People Proclaim. Susan has served over the years in multiple capacities and with multiple agencies to include Hospice by the Sea in Boca Raton and for 6 years was an 11th hour volunteer both at their care center and for people in their homes. Susan was a volunteer with Disaster Services of The American Red Cross, The American Association for Suicide Prevention and the Boca Raton Chamber of Commerce to name a few. Her advocacy and support of HIV/AIDS patients and families has been instrumental in helping many hurting people get through their personal stories of love and loss.

Susan's legacy includes having written several weekly motivational columns for the Boca Raton Newspaper and had been a guest speaker at the 2008 National Black HIV/AIDS Awareness Dinner (NBHAAD) held in West Palm Beach. Susan's abstinence only program was presented before the Women of Tomorrow Organization at Booker T. Washington Senior High School in Miami and throughout Florida. Susan was a volunteer with the Comprehensive AIDS Program of Palm Beach County, Real AIDS Prevention Program (RAPP), Area 9 Minority AIDS Network, and the Palm Beach County Substance Abuse Coalition (PBCSAC).

Susan's lecture series entitled "YOU DON'T GET AIDS FROM LOVING SOMEBODY" has been presented throughout South Florida as she speaks openly about abstinence and testing in order to stop the spread of this deadly disease. Susan gives her testimony before youth and single ministries, in high schools, churches, synagogues, organizations, and other venues in regard to HIV/AIDS testing, education, and awareness. Susan is still an HIV/AIDS advocate for testing and believes that mandatory legislation for testing of all STD's should be put in place.

Susan is available for on/off air interviews, speaking engagements and personal appearances.

Features/ Appearances

Susan has appeared on the 700 Club with Pat Robertson in a segment entitled "Till Death Do Us Part" and she has also been featured on TBN's Praise The Lord program. Susan was a contributing writer for Prophetess Cynthia Thompson's Women You Will Magazine which is geared to empowering, motivating, and educating women about issues important to women about women. Susan wrote a monthly cooking column entitled "Cooking With Yeshua" for the JPPIMC newsletter.

Susan legacy includes having written a weekly motivational column for the Boca Raton Newspaper and been a guest speaker at the 2008 National Black HIV/AIDS Awareness Dinner (NBHAAD) held in West Palm Beach. Susan's abstinence only program was presented before the Women of Tomorrow Organization at Booker T. Washington Senior High School in Miami and Florida. Susan was a volunteer with the Comprehensive AIDS Program of Palm Beach County, Real AIDS Prevention Program (RAPP), Urban 9

Minority AIDS Network, Palm Beach County Substance Abuse Coalition (PBCSAC), The American Foundation For Suicide Prevention, The American Red Cross and Hospice By The Sea in Boca Raton. Susan's lecture series entitled **"YOU DON'T GET AIDS FROM LOVING SOMEBODY"** has been presented throughout South Florida as she speaks openly about abstinence and testing in order to stop the spread of this deadly disease. Susan gives her testimony before youth and single ministries, in high schools, churches, synagogues, organizations, and other venues in regard to HIV/AIDS testing, education, and awareness. Susan is still an HIV/AIDS advocate for testing and believes that mandatory legislation for testing of all STD's should be put in place.

Susan's television appearances include: WPBF Channel 25-West Palm Beach, "Dealing With Menopause Through Weight Training"; WPTV Channel 5 -West Palm Beach-noon news live with Kelly Dunn, "Muscles, Menopause, and The Fabulous Fifties"; WRGB Channel 6 – Albany, New York, Noon News with Sue Nigra- "Bodybuilding For Baby Boomers"; WTEN Channel 10 – Albany, New York, Noon News with Tracy Egan – "Menopause and Muscles"; WNYT Channel 13 in Albany, New York in a segment on "Menopause and Bodybuilding for Baby Boomers"; Channel 23- Adelphia Cable for Lynn University in Boca Raton, Florida in the "Around Our Town" show hosted By Sid Snyder; WSVN Channel 7 in Miami, Florida for the show "Deco Drive;" "The Today Show" in Sydney, Australia; WXEL Public Television in West Palm Beach, Florida on the South Florida Today Show "Recovery After a Loved One's Loss" and "Healthy Cooking"; WPBT Public Television in Miami, Florida for Bill Moyer's Special – "On Our Own Terms" and "How Volunteering For Hospice Helped During The Recovery Process"; WPLG Channel 10 in Miami/Fort Lauderdale, Florida on

"New Years Resolutions" – Sticking To An Exercise Program and "The Benefits of Weight Training During Menopause."

Her radio interviews and guest appearances include: WRMB – Moody Bible Radio–Boynton Beach, Florida-talk show host Dana Shelton; The True Christian Club of Boynton Beach Community High School; Jesus People Proclaim International Ministries Church, Boca Raton, Florida-youth ministry and congregation; WFTL-1400 Talk Radio; "The Sunday Morning Magazine Show" with Peg Browning on The Gator Radio Network, and The Coast Radio Morning Show with Terri Griffin. These interviews included questions concerning her marriage and AIDS. Daily newspapers and monthly magazines have printed articles about Susan including those appearing in: *The Jewish Star Times, Natural Awakenings, The Boca Raton News, The South Florida Sun-Sentinel, The Happy Times Newspaper, and Vital Signs Magazine* (South Florida's #1 Resource Guide to Nurses and Health Care Professionals) in a question and answer column titled "The Benefits of Bodybuilding During Menopause." She also wrote a column in the *Boca Raton News* titled "With a Hospice Heart," and serves as a contributing writer and columnist for *Natural MuscleMagazine, Michael Body Scenes Magazine,* and *The Boca Del Mar Newsletter*.

Susan has spoken at the following Bookstores in South Florida about her lecture series entitled "You Don't Get AIDS From Loving Somebody." Borders Books and Music, Barnes and Noble Bookstores, and Liberties Books in Mizner Park and Ft. Lauderdale . Her speaking engagements for non-profit organizations in South Florida include: Hadassah, ORT, City of Hope , Women's Clubs, Condominium Associations, Civic Groups, BocaCares, Professional Women's Organizations, Hospice By The Sea, The Comprehensive

AIDS Program of Palm Beach County and the Adolph & Rose Levis Jewish Community Center (JCC).

Susan was featured as a guest lecturer and keynote speaker at the following events: North Broward Regional Medical Center-Health Fair, Expos, and Seminars; Women Health Fairs and Seminars at the Boca Raton Community Hospital, West Boca Community Hospital, CAP, and the JCC. The Comprehensive AIDS Program has featured Susan as a keynote speaker for its annual Walk For Life in West Palm Beach, Florida and at numerous fundraisers where she signs her cookbook, "Safe Sex Never Tasted So Good." Hospice by the Sea in Boca Raton has her on its Speakers' Bureau. Susan represents Hospice at health fairs, educational seminars, local hospitals, and at events like the Boca Expo, The Delray Affair, workshops, and vending booths at local malls.

PERSONAL BACKGROUND
Once a professional dental hygienist, Susan married her elementary-school sweetheart, **Jeffrey**, at the age of 22. Their marriage was passionate and full of ups and downs with the surprising revelation that Jeffrey was bi-sexual. Her enduring love and unconditional acceptance for Jeffrey during this difficult period never wavered. For 25 years, Susan kept her commitment to their marriage. In June 1992, Jeffrey was diagnosed with AIDS. She rallied with him in the fight for his life. On August 17, 1994, Jeffrey passed away in the privacy of their home with the help of hospice. Jeffrey's death left Susan searching for comfort and support which she later found through writing, exercise, cooking, and her faith.

Susan's proclivity towards nutrition developed into a penchant for cooking. She began cooking up a storm relying upon her humor and motivational attitude while pleasing palates everywhere. Her recipes were healthy, creative, easy-to-prepare and flavorful with off-color and shockingly unique names. She penned these and other recipes into a renowned cookbook titled "Safe Sex Never Tasted So Good" with partial proceeds benefiting non-profit organizations. Cooking enabled Susan to make a positive and immediate impact in the lives of others through nutrition.

Susan pursued her cooking with passion and was forced to further challenge her culinary skills when she began weight training. Her discipline motivated many people who she influenced and taught through personal training in the South Florida area. When Susan isn't writing, cooking, or working out, she contributed her time and efforts through her volunteer work and community involvement. At Hospice by the Sea, she served as an 11th hour volunteer–one who is called when a patient's death is imminent-and educates others about AIDS through the Comprehensive AIDS Program (CAP) of Palm Beach County, Florida.

Other Books & Info

Author • Speaker • Advocate • Philanthropist

Contact Susan
www.SusanMintz.com
Email: smintz7179@aol.com Phone: 561-271-1879
Facebook: Susan Mintz

And I Held their Hands with a Hospice Heart
- Stories of Hope, Faith, Love and Loss

Book Ordering Information:

$22.95 Paperback // $12ea for Bulk orders of 25+

$9.95 eBook

Order at **www.PurposePublishing.com**

Leave comments at Susan **www.SusanMintz.com**

Other Titles

Committed to Love
A Woman's Journey through Love and Loss

Book Ordering Information:

$26.95 Hardback

$22.95 Paperback // $12ea for Bulk orders of 25+

$9.95 eBook

Coming Soon

Cooking with Yeshua

www.ingramcontent.com/pod-product-compliance
Lightning Source LLC
Chambersburg PA
CBHW062012180426
43199CB00034B/2411